Rousseau and the Paradox of Alienation

Rousseau and the Paradox of Alienation

Sally Howard Campbell

LEXINGTON BOOKS
Lanham • Boulder • New York • Toronto • Plymouth, UK

Published by Lexington Books
A wholly owned subsidiary of The Rowman & Littlefield Publishing Group, Inc.
4501 Forbes Boulevard, Suite 200, Lanham, Maryland 20706
www.rowman.com

Estover Road, Plymouth PL6 7PY, United Kingdom

British Library Cataloguing in Publication Information Available

Library of Congress Cataloging-in-Publication Data

Campbell, Sally Howard, 1963–
Rousseau and the paradox of alienation / Sally Howard Campbell.
pages cm
Includes bibliographical references.
ISBN 978-0-7391-6632-1 (cloth : alk. paper)—ISBN 978-0-7391-6634-5 (electronic book)
1. Rousseau, Jean-Jacques, 1712–1778. 2. Alienation (Philosophy) I. Title.
B2138.A55C36 2012
302.5'44—dc23
2011048962

I would rather be a man of paradoxes than a man of prejudices.

—Jean-Jacques Rousseau, *Émile*

Contents

Acknowledgments

Because this book began as my doctoral dissertation, I must thank those who helped me through that part of the process. John Scott has been generous with his ideas and advice from the project's inception to its present form. My debt to him is great. Donald Lutz was particularly helpful to me as I worked on the final chapters, but more importantly it was in his undergraduate class that I first realized my love of political theory. In addition, thank you to Cynthia Freeland and the late Ross Lence for their time and thoughtful comments.

Thank you to Marshall for making the starting of this project possible, and to Vaughn for making the finishing of it matter.

This book is dedicated to my mom and dad.

Preface

Rousseau's thought is a pivotal point in the history of the concept of alienation. In his writings one finds the bridge between the now-dominant psychosocial interpretation and the legal-political interpretation that prevailed prior to his writings. Rousseau's transformation of the concept is prepared in the works of Grotius, Hobbes, and Locke, whose writings link the inalienability of certain rights to those characteristics considered essential to one's being as a moral agent. Furthermore, Rousseau's writings lay much of the groundwork for Marx's more explicit discussions of man's alienation.

Rousseau's *Discourse on the Origin and Foundations of Inequality* depicts the development of man's awareness of himself as a conscious and moral being. Rousseau illustrates man's historical journey from a natural state of self-sufficiency to one of dependence and alienation. In his later writings (primarily *Emile* and *The Social Contract*), Rousseau considers both an individual and a political remedy to the degeneration of man's condition. The individual remedy consists of carefully educating the young child and protecting him from the corrupting influences of society until his character is sufficiently developed. In the political solution, which I examine here, Rousseau paradoxically determines that it is through man's total alienation of himself that he can be restored to a state of wholeness, free from the alienating effects of civil society. Under Rousseau's social contract, a true community emerges when the interests of men and the interests of the community can be merged into one.

This work is unique because little of the literature on alienation recognizes the influential role played by Rousseau's writings. Through careful analysis it is shown here that the themes of self-alienation and alienation from others, most often credited to the writings of Marx, are clearly laid out by Rousseau. Like Marx, Rousseau is concerned with man's separation from his natural state, he considers the advent of the division of labor to be a critical step in the development of man's alienation, and he believes that alienation can be transcended through the merging of the individual and the community.

Introduction

The idea of man's alienation from himself and from others has, over time, been addressed by thinkers in theology, philosophy, political theory, sociology, psychology, and other fields. The now-prevalent psychosocial notion of alienation is most often attributed to Marx and traced through him to Hegel, and is rarely recognized as having existed beforehand. But the concept of alienation did exist before Hegel and Marx, and it is in the works of Jean-Jacques Rousseau that it underwent a transformation from a purely legal-political notion to one with great psychological and social significance.

This work demonstrates that the concept of alienation is not substantially different as discussed by Rousseau and Marx, and that what is commonly traced back to Marx might be more accurately traced back to Rousseau. Rousseau not only addresses the alienation of property and sovereignty (as had the writings of many before him), but also develops the idea of social and self-alienation in a way that heavily influences subsequent thought. Rousseau describes modern, social man as a being at odds with his own true, independent nature and isolated from those around him. Human relationships are hindered by the "false veil of politeness" that masks men's true feelings. Marx's own development of the psychosocial notion of alienation is predicated upon the transformation of the idea affected by Rousseau. As Gauthier notes, "[t]he idea of 'sociable man, always outside of himself' is the forerunner of the alienated worker in Marx" (2006, 25). Addressing the way in which Rousseau brought forth a new understanding of individual unity and social relationships, this book will further illuminate discussions of the origins of estrangement from one's true self and from one's fellow humans.

Indeed, the most common contemporary understanding of the concept of alienation is as a psychological condition of estrangement and disaffection. We think of the alienated person as alone in a crowd, unable to connect to others and perhaps unnoticed by them. The modern conception of alienation is characterized by the irony of feeling isolated and lonely in the midst of the flow of society.[1] Alienation is doubly ironic when suffered by Rousseau's modern man. Rousseau believed man in his natural state to be asocial, isolated, and content. Lacking both self-consciousness and a conscious awareness of others, he hadn't the capacity for alienation. Unfortunately, it is the same developments that make man aware of himself and of others that eventually make him feel disconnected from both.

In the writings of natural law thinkers such as Grotius, Hobbes, and Locke, alienation referred to the transfer of one's proprietary or political powers. These thinkers deemed certain rights to be inalienable because they were essential characteristics of one's being as a moral agent and, therefore, could not be renounced. If the way that a theorist conceives of alienation (what is alienable, what is not) is dependent upon what is considered to be fundamental to the human being, then a transformation in the conception of alienation must be predicated on a transformation in the conception of what makes one human. Each of the above theorists, in fact, broadened the list of attributes considered fundamental to the human being, and with this came a broadening of the list of inalienable rights. For Rousseau, those elements from which one cannot reasonably and healthily be separated extend well beyond life and liberty. One must also preserve one's spirit—one's *self*. Rousseau's development of the idea of alienation from one's self and from others indicates a belief that what makes one human is influenced by social configurations. By broadening this understanding of what makes one human and the social and historical forces that influence human development, Rousseau allows for the introduction of the psychosocial conception of alienation. The articulation of this concept made it possible for Rousseau and others after him to describe the social, political, and economic conditions under which man's material needs may be met, and in which he may believe himself to be content, but under which he is, in fact, deprived of the unity of self that is a crucial component to human happiness.

In both the *Discourse on the Origin and Foundations of Inequality* (*Second Discourse*) and *The Social Contract* (*SC*), Rousseau discusses alienation in the legal-political sense of Hobbes and Locke. In the *Second Discourse*, Rousseau states that, regarding property, "every man can dispose of at will what he possesses." As for life and freedom, however, "it would offend both nature and reason to renounce them whatever the price" (*Second Discourse*, 168). In *The Social Contract*, Rousseau speaks of the inalienability of one's liberty, and also of that which must be alienated in the establishment of civil society (*SC*, I.4, I.6). In addition to this legal-political usage of the concept, however, Rousseau speaks, though not by name, of alienation from one's self and from others in a way that had not previously been done. According to Rousseau, humans in the state of nature are entirely independent. They are complete and self-sufficient. They have only the simplest needs (food, shelter, sex), which are easily met without the formation of enduring relationships. Pre-social beings are "subject to few passions and self-sufficient" (*Second Discourse*, 137). The coming together of individuals to form communities, however, ends this independence and self-sufficiency. As humans form relationships with one another, they become dependent upon these relationships. Yack

(1992) accurately identifies the resultant loss of one's independence as the reason for Rousseau's contempt for modern society, but he does not discuss the alienating effects of this loss. It is too simplistic to say that the savage *enjoys* independence; it is independence that allows him to be whole.

The personal dependence that civil society fosters is twofold. Individuals become dependent on the conveniences and ease of living provided by a division of labor and, more importantly, they become psychologically dependent on the recognition and esteem of those around them. The formation of communities creates a division of labor in families and in the community as a whole. Rousseau considered the division of labor to separate individuals from the source of their existence in much the same way that Marx later considered the creation of wages to separate individuals from the product of their labor. In both cases, man experiences a loss of independence and wholeness. As Gauthier writes, "[F]or Rousseau, as later for Marx, the primary effect of the division of labor is . . . to enslave [men] by making the exercise of their own capacities dependent on their fellows' alien wills" (2006, 14). Formerly independent men now find themselves bound to others and once self-sufficient beings have become soft and weak and are both unwilling and unable to do without that which has enabled them to achieve a more comfortable way of life. This dependence on ease and plenty is self-perpetuating. As humans grow accustomed to their softer life, they begin to view those things that make it possible as needs, rather than as luxuries, or even conveniences.

As with many who have written on the relationship between Rousseau and Marx, Horowitz emphasizes the Marxian aspects of Rousseau's writings, but to stress the role of economic factors as a cause of alienation is to underestimate the importance of the psychological aspect. Horowitz discusses the alienating effects of the division of labor as described by Rousseau in the *Second Discourse* and, painting Rousseau as somewhat of a proto-Marxist, places heavy emphasis on the role of money in the emergent division of labor. According to Horowitz's interpretation, the primacy of exchange relations in civil society creates forms of interest and duty that are antithetical and that result in one of the ways in which "the existence of men in civil society is alienated, fragmented and at odds with itself" (1987, 121). Horowitz's emphasis on the economic origin of alienation, however, is more appropriately applied to Marx than to Rousseau. It is the effects of civil society on the social and psychological facets of human beings that Rousseau himself emphasizes, and it is on these that I will focus my attention. Furthermore, these social and psychological facets are not absent in the writings of Marx. Though Marx stressed the economic *causes* of man's alienation, the alienation itself is not economic but psychological and social in nature.

Though the division of labor creates a material dependence among humans, the more important way in which individuals become dependent is through the newly acquired consciousness of one's self as a human being. This nascent self-consciousness results not only in the ability to compare one's self to others, but in the inability *not* to. Such comparisons allow for the introduction and appreciation of esteem. It soon becomes "necessary to appear to be other than what one in fact was. To be and to seem to be became two altogether different things" (*Second Discourse*, 155–56). Individuals soon feel the need for esteem as powerfully as the need for food and shelter, and their dependence on others deepens. As Rousseau writes: "the savage lives within himself; the social man, always outside himself, knows how to live only in the opinion of others; and it is, so to speak, from their judgment alone that he draws the sentiment of his own existence" (*Second Discourse*, 179).

That individuals in civil society are quite different from their pre-civil state is clear. The divergence between the real and the apparent begins almost immediately upon the acquisition of self-consciousness and the recognition that one has an "appearance." As soon as humans are aware *that* they are perceived by others, they desire to control *how* they are perceived. This split between the real and the apparent was, for Rousseau, symbolic of the split between real and false individuals. In his analysis of the roles of appearance and reality, Starobinski touches on Rousseau's view of one's alienation from one's self: "[T]he gap between appearance and reality marks the triumph of the "factitious," the ever-growing disparity not only between ourselves and the outside world but between ourselves and our own inner nature" (1988, 27). Focusing largely on the relationship between Rousseau's life and his writings, Starobinski does not go on to explore the separation of the individual from his inner nature in great detail. The impact of this separation, however, was of great concern to Rousseau. The psychological consequences of such an existence are well described by Allan Bloom in *Love and Friendship*:

> A being concerned only with himself has to spend his time worrying about the intentions of others and trying to hide his own from them, threatening, flattering, lying. In his selfishness, he forgets himself. His soul goes wandering out over the world of men and never returns, while he becomes hypocritical, envious, vain, slavish, measuring himself relative to the success or failure of others. This is the condition of alienation. (1993, 48–49)

Civil life, thus, changes one from an independent, self-sufficient, and solitary being to one that is dependent, prideful and plagued by needs that must be satisfied. One's very nature has been altered, and the former self is hardly visible. We now have "original man vanishing by degrees . . . an assemblage of artificial men and factitious passions which are the work of all these new relations and have no true foundation in nature" (*Second Discourse*, 178). In civil society, one's needs, passions, and emotions are conventional and false. Beings in the state of nature and civil beings are alien to one another, as if they are of different species. Civil society takes the savage in the state of nature, who was entirely human, and requires him to be a citizen, but because the virtues and obligations of humans and citizens are not only different but often incompatible, civil society creates a being in constant conflict with itself. Neither wholly human nor wholly citizen, civil men are fractured and dissonant (see *Emile*, 40–41).

Rousseau remains hopeful that, with the advent of proper social institutions, the human situation might be improved if, perhaps, not restored to its previous state. In *The Social Contract*, Rousseau describes a civil society that would restore equality and unity to men. Here he takes alienation through somewhat of a second transformation—from the problem to the solution. In doing so, Rousseau sets up an interesting paradox: his prescribed remedy for the alienation of the individual is the alienation of all that the individual is and possesses. Rousseau determines that it is only through the total alienation of one's self to the community that one can be restored to completeness. According to Shklar, Rousseau depicts the society of his day as one, "that has destroyed man's original inner unity," and only under Rousseau's social contract do we find, "a society in which men are restored to inner and outer unity through the triumph of the social and moral will" (1957, 28). Similarly, Yack's analysis of Rousseau states that, "Modern institutions produce only divided souls. . . . Only institutions that can restore the wholeness individuals lost in entering the social state . . . are not worthless in Rousseau's eyes" (1992, 53). The goal of the social contract is, in Rousseau's words, to "find a form of association which defends and protects with all common forces the person and goods of each associate, and by means of which each one, while uniting with all, nevertheless obeys only himself and remains as free as before" (*SC*, I.6). Under Rousseau's social contract, each individual merges his own interests into those of the larger group and, under these conditions, a true community emerges. This is now possible because the creation of the social contract has led to the creation of true citizens. Without the social contract, there exists perpetual conflict between the interests of the individual and the interests of the community. By truly uniting all individuals into a community, however, the social contract makes these interests coterminous. Melzer argues, "[T]he new self or unity thus produced is a new kind of self. It is no longer a "sensuous" or "natural" self based on what one desires and is, but a "moral" and "ideal" self based on what one wills and respects" (1980, 1031). The aim of the social contract goes well beyond providing the security and justice of political and social organization. As Yack writes, "[I]n demanding the alienation of the individual to the community, Rousseau seeks to legitimize and make tolerable the chains of dependence that we must bear in civil society. . . . he demands the complete subordination of the individual *for the sake of the individual*" (1992, 63; emphasis original). The social contract aims to create a form of organized society that approximates the original conditions of independence and unity for otherwise alienated individuals.

Rousseau paints for us a clear picture of the human individual: whole and independent in nature, but painfully divided under present social conditions. It is these social conditions that are at the root of the individual's loss of unity. Similarly, Marx outlines the economic and social conditions to which he attributes the individual's alienated state. Although Marx's discussions of alienation focus on the economic causes, both Rousseau and Marx are dealing with social and individual problems brought about by the conditions of modern society. For Marx, the root of the problem can be distilled down to the development of wage labor. Whereas individuals once worked to provide directly their means for existence, under wage labor they are forced to work for pay. The product of one's labor is no longer directly linked to one's being. Human beings are thus alienated from the product of their labor, their productive activity, their fellow humans and themselves. This alienation stemming from the means of production leads one to experience a loss of self almost identical to that described by Rousseau.

Marx's debt to Rousseau is not, however, limited to their similar theories of the individual's inner division. There are parallels in the general aspects of their theories, as well. Marx, like Rousseau, had a great appreciation for the influence of historical and social forces on human nature and development. Furthermore, though Marx does not adopt Rousseau's remedy of dealienation through alienation, he does see a social remedy to the problem. In much the same way that Rousseau's social contract transcends the alienation brought about by civil society, Marx's communist state transcends the alienation brought about by wage labor. In both cases, a restructuring of social, political, and economic relationships is prescribed.

Though much has been written on the independent topics of Rousseau and alienation, little has been written about the meeting of the two. Very little of what has been written on the psychosocial notion of alienation recognizes its existence prior to the writings of Hegel. Furthermore, although comparisons have previously been drawn between Rousseau and Marx, those that mention the common theme of alienation do so only in a cursory manner. Marx's discussions of alienation are, in fact, heavily dependent upon Rousseau's transformation of the concept from legal-political to psychosocial. This work aims to provide a careful and concise examination of the role of alienation in Rousseau's political and social philosophy, as well as the role of Rousseau in the history of alienation as a concept.

NOTE

1. One has to suspect that Rousseau would be particularly horrified by the impact of current technology and social media on our sense of ourselves and our relationships with others. Is a Facebook status or a Twitter message really an expression of our inner self, or are we caught up in a now-constant need to create clever reflections of ourselves for widespread consumption by people that we barely know? The "false veil of civility" that so concerned Rousseau in his own day has now been extended to include being "friended" by people that we have met once and may never see again. Surely Rousseau would argue that the hyperreflective, hyperconnected society we now inhabit is only driving us further from ourselves and from others. That from which we seem to draw the sentiment of our modern existence (how many "likes" our last Facebook post garnered or how many followers we have on Twitter) is becoming *de*creasingly meaningful.

ONE

Alienation Prior to Rousseau

Rousseau's thought is a pivotal point in the history of the concept of alienation, and it is in his writings that one finds the bridge between the psychosocial interpretation of alienation that has been dominant since the early nineteenth century, and the legal-political interpretation that was in common usage prior to Rousseau. Although Rousseau does not use the term "alienation" to describe man's loss of wholeness, his writings prepare the later use of the term in this context. As Gauthier writes, "[w]hatever one makes of the idea that contemporary Western society alienates the individual from his true nature, Rousseau was the first, I think, to express it" (2006, xi).

In the writings of natural law thinkers such as Grotius, Hobbes, and Locke, alienation refers to the transfer of one's proprietary and/or political powers. Rousseau addresses the works of each of these writers in the early part of *The Social Contract*. He criticizes Grotius and Hobbes together for what he perceives as their belief in the legitimacy of the alienation of one's liberty, resulting in, "the human race belong[ing] to a hundred men" (*SC*, I.2). Without mentioning Locke by name, Rousseau echoes his argument that men are born to freedom and, upon reaching maturity, are no longer the subjects of parental authority (*SC*, I.2). I will elaborate on each of these arguments momentarily, however, the importance of these writers to an examination of Rousseau's beliefs on inalienability is not due solely to the fact that Rousseau refers to their work, nor is it due to their conclusions regarding what is or is not alienable. Their greatest relevance to this discussion stems from the way in which their conclusions regarding inalienability were drawn. Beginning in the works of Grotius, one sees the establishment of a relationship between what is inalienable and what is fundamental to man as a moral being. Those rights that are essential characteristics of one's being as a moral agent are

1

inalienable not simply because renunciation would be inadvisable, but because it would leave man less than fully human.

As the standard for determining alienability, this criterion has also served as the source of its evolution. If the way that a theorist conceives of alienation (what is alienable, what is not) is dependent upon what is considered to be fundamental to the human being, then a transformation in the conception of alienation must be predicated on a transformation in the conception of what makes one human. Rousseau's development of the idea of alienation from one's self and from others, then, indicates a belief that what makes man human is influenced by (if not dependent upon) social configurations. It is this broadening of the understanding of personhood and the forces that constitute the person that then allows for the introduction of the psychosocial conception of alienation. Furthermore, it is Rousseau's concern for man as a human being, and not merely as a political being, that leads him to design the social contract. As will be discussed in greater depth later, the total alienation of the social contract is a response to the psychological division that plagues man in modern civil society.

GROTIUS

In the early pages of *The Social Contract*, Rousseau makes several references to the writings of Hugo Grotius. Rousseau criticizes Grotius's view of the world as divided up into "so many herds of cattle, each with its own ruler" resulting in "the human race belong[ing] to a hundred men" (*SC*, I.2). Grotius's view, as Rousseau perceives it, of the many belonging to the few, is at odds with Rousseau's insistence that men suffer when made to depend on others. An important source of this tension between the theories of Grotius and Rousseau is the former's willingness to distinguish personal freedom from political sovereignty. Rousseau allows for no such separation and it is this that prepares the transformation of certain concepts in his theory.

In *The Jurisprudence of Holland*, Grotius writes, "[t]hings belonging to individuals are by nature alienable or inalienable. Inalienable things are things which belong so essentially to one man that they could not belong to another, as a man's life, body, freedom, honor. . . . Alienable things are things which by their nature can belong to one person as well as to another. Such things are commonly called 'goods' or 'possessions.'" (*JofH*, 41; 42; 49). Although Grotius makes clear the inalienability of freedom here, his position on the subject is less clear elsewhere. In *The Rights of War and Peace*,[1] it seems that Grotius considers the voluntary surrender of one's independence to be legitimate under certain circumstances. Subjection is defined as either private (surrender of an individual) or public (surrender of a people). Though Grotius calls slavery the "basest form of voluntary subjection," he goes on to say that, under suitable circumstances, slavery is not "intolerably bitter" and, in fact, provides one with "the perpetual assurance of maintenance, which often those who work for daily hire do not have" (*W&P*, 2.5.27). Furthermore, masters do not enjoy "rights of life and death over their slaves" (*W&P*, 2.5.28). The slavery that Grotius describes here does not sound as much like the alienation of one's freedom as it does a business contract. It does not appear to be a case of one man's unconditional ownership of another. It is essentially an exchange of labor for support, executed on a long-term basis.

Rousseau not only disagrees with the premise that one may make oneself slave to another, but he also finds Grotius's logic to be flawed for the following reason: a man who makes himself a slave receives (at least) his subsistence in return. A people who make themselves subjects, however, receive no such compensation from their king. They alienate their freedom to no benefit. In fact, argues Rousseau, it is the king who gains his subsistence from his subjects. In his discussion on slavery in *The Social Contract*, Rousseau writes, "[i]f an individual, says Grotius, can alienate his liberty and make himself the slave of a master, why could not a whole people do the same and make itself subject to a king?" (*SC*, I.4). Given Rousseau's definition of alienation as "to give or to sell," both of which one assumes to be voluntary actions, the alienation of a people to a king would not be a logical act. There is nothing to be gained by a people from alienating (or "selling") themselves into subjection (*SC*, I.4). Although Grotius does not elaborate on the subjection of a people to a king, as he does on the subjection of a slave to a master, he speaks of such public subjection in a similarly dispassionate tone, stating, "[i]t is public subjection when a people surrenders itself to a man or to several men or to another people" (*W&P*, 2.5.31). In a discussion of the alienation of sovereignty just prior to this section, Grotius first establishes that what is (fully) owned can be alienated, and then outlines the conditions under which the sovereignty of a person or a people can be alienated. These conditions are unambiguous and unexceptional. For example, one part of a body of people cannot elect to alienate the sovereignty of all (one's sovereignty cannot be alienated against one's will), and a part cannot withdraw from the whole (through alienation of sovereignty) except under dire circumstances (*W&P*, 2.6). More pragmatic than philosophical in tone, this discussion has no clear relationship to the earlier discussions of the inalienability of freedom. There is nothing to indicate that Grotius considered the relationship between subjects and their king to be unjust or against the law of nature.

One answer to Grotius's apparent lack of clarity on the issue of freedom and slavery may lie in his complex definition of property, which entails the use or possession of something but *not necessarily* the power of alienating it (see *W&P*, 1.1.5; Tully 1980, 112). Given this definition, a man may have only use rights over his freedom, allowing him to give these rights over to a master but preventing him from giving over wholesale ownership, a right which he himself does not possess. This limited definition of ownership is exemplified in Grotius's discussion of inalienability in *The Jurisprudence of Holland*. A man's freedom, for example, belongs to him, "so that he may protect and use it." He may *not*, however, "entirely dispose of his freedom by contract" (*JofH*, 47). That this is a discussion of "[t]hings *belonging to* individuals" (*JofH*, 41; emphasis added) illustrates that, for Grotius, one may possess something and yet have only limited rights to it.

It appears, from the very different ways in which Grotius addresses the inalienability of freedom and the alienability of political sovereignty, that he considered them to be quite separate. This, of course, becomes a point of contention for Rousseau, for whom the two were quite intimately and inextricably connected. Grotius's use of both *a priori* and *a posteriori* methodology accounts for some apparent contradiction in his position and is one source of Rousseau's dissatisfaction with his (Grotius's) theory. On the relevance of both methods, Grotius states:

> The existence of the Law of Nature is proved by two kinds of argument, *a priori* and *a posteriori*, the former a more abstruse, and the latter a more popular method of proof. We are said to reason *a priori*, when we show agreement or disagreement of any thing with a reasonable and social nature; but *a posteriori*, when without absolute proof, but only upon probability, any thing is inferred to accord with the law of nature, because it is received as such among all, or at least the more civilized nations. (*W&P*, 1.1.12)

Rousseau criticizes Grotius for his habit of establishing "right by fact" (*SC*, I.4), but Grotius justifies his use of historical evidence as a necessary additional source, stating that, "whatever cannot be deduced from certain principles by a sure process of reasoning, and yet is clearly observed everywhere, must have its origin in the free will of man" (*Prolegomena*, 40). If the principles of the law of nature, which are "manifest and clear," led Grotius to conclude that one's freedom (among other things) is inalienable, then what is to be said of the historical examples of slavery and subjection? It may be from these factual examples that Grotius draws his conclusion that, under proper conditions, the slave is compensated for his servitude and thus, "within natural limits, [slavery] contains nothing that in itself is intolerably bitter" (*W&P*, 2.5.27). The same may be true for Grotius's discussion of the alienability of sovereignty. The fit between the *a priori* and the *a posteriori* is not exact, and Grotius's method of drawing from them both may account for some apparent discrepancies in his theory. Rousseau similarly accuses Grotius of basing principles on the authority of poets, but Grotius was careful to explain that the testimony of "philosophers, historians, poets and orators" is used only to substantiate what has already been concluded. Furthermore, he defends the use of testimony by those who, though far flung in time and place, "affirm the same thing as certain." Such conclusions are necessarily viable either as "a correct conclusion drawn from the principles of nature, or common consent" (*Prolegomena*, 40).

The significance of Grotius's writings on alienation, however, extends beyond the fact that they were read and critiqued by Rousseau. A relationship emerges in the works of Grotius that is picked up by those who follow him and truly solidified by Rousseau. First, Grotius points to the existence of distinct and identifiable categories regarding alienability and inalienability. These categories are neither arbitrary nor time-bound, and all things will fit into one or the other. Second, in outlining these categories, Grotius makes explicit the relationship between inalienability and the essential elements of personhood. In the realm of "things" that can be considered to *belong to* an individual (and for Grotius, this is quite inclusive), it is those characteristics fundamental to the human being that one cannot renounce.

When Grotius states that, "[i]nalienable things are things which belong so essentially to one man that they could not belong to another, as a man's life, body, freedom, honour" (*JofH*, 42), he establishes an important theme that appears in the examinations of inalienable rights by those who follow him—that what is inalienable to man is not determined by external social or legal factors, but by internal ones. In other words, what one considers to be an inalienable right may have little to do with guidelines set forth by laws or governing bodies. It may have only to do with those characteristics that make men moral beings and thus separate them from all others. It is not a question of what is socially appropriate or legally allowable but rather a question of what is humanly possible.

HOBBES

Rousseau considers Hobbes, like Grotius, to be too ready to see men alienate their sovereignty. In *The Social Contract*, Rousseau includes Hobbes as one who believes that "the human race belongs to a hundred men" (*SC*, I.2). Hobbes's beliefs on the alienation of rights stem from his beliefs about man in the state of nature. Hobbes's state of nature is characterized by the common right that all men have to all things. Several factors, however, complicate this right. It is inevitable that there will be occasions when two or more individuals desire the same thing. If they each possess equal right to it and there is no mechanism (i.e., governing authority) for determining who shall have it, then it is hard to imagine a nonviolent resolution. It is the inevitability of circumstances such as this that led Hobbes to conclude in *De Cive* that, "it was the least benefit for men thus to have a common right to all things. For the effects of this right are the same, almost, as if there had been no right at all" (I.11). What good, in other words, is the right to something when one must nonetheless compete for it with all his fellow right-holders? A mutual right to all things is, in effect, a right to nothing. With no governing authority and thus no hope for establishing whose right might precede, there is no less conflict (and perhaps more) than if there were no right at all.

It is due to this pervasive potential for violent conflict that men seek some common power. According to Hobbes, men turn to the laws of nature to serve as their guide as they seek a more secure and peaceful way of life. Though Hobbes lists a number of natural laws, it is the first two with which I am most concerned. Hobbes understands the *fundamental law of nature* to be that men seek peace to the greatest degree possible. Having established that the state of nature is not naturally inclined toward peace, Hobbes's second law of nature instructs man, "*as far-forth as for peace and defence of himself he shall think it necessary, to lay down this right to all things, and be contented with so much liberty against other men, as he would allow other men against himself*" (*Leviathan*, xiv.5; emphasis original). By this dictum, Hobbes has established that men must relinquish some of their natural right to all things in order to create a civil society. It is this that leads to a more general discussion of the alienability of rights.

According to Hobbes, to divest oneself of one's rights, either through renunciation or through transfer, is a voluntary act, and "of the voluntary acts of every man the object is some *good to himself*. And therefore, there be some rights which no man can be understood by any words or other signs to have abandoned or transferred" (*Leviathan*, xiv.8; emphasis original). This passage indicates that there are some rights the renunciation or transfer of which *cannot* bring good, therefore one *could not* (choose to) renounce or transfer them. In other words, according to Hobbes's logic, if the dispossession of certain rights could hold *no possible* benefit for man, then those rights must be inalienable.

Among these inalienable rights is the right to resist death, assault, or imprisonment (the latter two may be reasonably suspected of leading to death). Given that Hobbes's right of nature is essentially man's right to resist death by any means necessary (as indicated by reason and judgment), then the renunciation of this right to resist would mean the renunciation of the right of nature—of what nature has bestowed upon man by virtue of his being human. As Polin has pointed out, this right of nature is at once man's right and man's nature and as such, cannot be separated from him. Man's natural right to self-preservation is such a clear and profound part of man's being that to articulate it as Hobbes does is simply "'the acknowledgment' of a fact." Based on man's "capacity to act according to reason and to govern oneself according to one's own rationally established judgment," this right is necessarily and exclusively human (Polin 1967, 18). In *De Cive*, Hobbes states that *right* signifies "that liberty which every man hath to make use of his natural faculties according to right reason. Therefore the first foundation of natural right is this, that *every man as much as in him lies endeavor to protect his life and members"* (*De Cive*, I.7). Man's right to self-preservation is bestowed upon him by nature and cannot be taken from him by civil society. Hobbes, like Grotius, deems inalienable that which is inextricable from man's existence *as an individual*. Man's ability to utilize the faculties of reason and judgment in his pursuit of a safe and comfortable life are exclusively man's, and to strip him of the right to do so would be to reduce him to something less than human.

Hobbes has expanded on those features that are instrumental to personhood and he has thus expanded on those rights that are inalienable. The rights that man may (perhaps *must*) retain upon entering civil society go beyond those necessary for mere survival. Hobbes contends that, although it is necessary for men seeking peace to lay down certain rights, they must retain such rights as "to govern their own bodies, [right to] enjoy air, water, motion, ways to go from place to place, and all things else without which a man cannot live, *or not live well"* (*Leviathan*, xv.22; emphasis added; see Polin 18–19). With this declaration comes a significant step in the evolution of man's inalienable rights. Hobbes has broadened the realm of inalienable rights beyond what man needs to stay alive and includes what man needs to "live well." A certain standard of living is now a necessary ingredient for the full realization of personhood. What may have been present in Grotius's inclusion of freedom and honor as essential characteristics of man has now been articulated by Hobbes— that natural right entitles man to a certain *quality* of life. That this is left relatively undefined is in keeping with Hobbes's belief that what is good must be determined by each man individually. The scope of inalienable rights has now been rendered somewhat open-ended. Hobbes leaves men to determine for themselves that without which they cannot live well and, therefore, that which makes them whole and human beings. The primary passions that unite men as moral beings are the fear of violent death and the desire for a comfortable life. It is around the avoidance of the former and the securing of the latter that Hobbes has built his theory of inalienable rights.

LOCKE

Though there is intense disagreement in the theories of Rousseau and Locke regarding the role of property, they share common ground in their beliefs regarding freedom and equality.[2] Rousseau and Locke both believe that freedom and equality are natural conditions for men. Rousseau supported Locke's disagreement with Filmer's doctrine of "fatherly authority," which contends that men are born into subjection and are thus not naturally free (*First Treatise*, 6). It is Locke's belief that, although "[c]hildren . . . are not born in this full state of *equality* . . . they are born to it" (*Second Treatise*, VI.55; emphasis original). Echoing Locke, Rousseau considered the child to be under the authority of the father only as long as survival warrants, after which child and father "return equally to independence" (*SC*, I.2). As children grow older and reason develops, they come to enjoy full equality with others and freedom from parental authority.

Locke's belief in man's natural freedom from the authority of other men forms the cornerstone of much of his thought. The end of law (the law of nature) is not to restrict man's freedom but to enlarge and protect it. Of man in civil society, Locke writes, "*where there is no law, there is no freedom: for liberty is, to be free from restraint and violence from others; which cannot be where there is no law*" (*Second Treatise*, VI.57; emphasis original). The natural freedom to which men are born (and which they attain upon adulthood) is not freedom to live entirely without a guiding force. It is rather a man's freedom to live his life and pursue his desires restricted only by the law of nature (*Second Treatise*, IV.22). The law of nature will prevent man from following a path that would put his life and freedom in extreme danger.

Locke defines the law of nature as reason, and reason leads man to act in the interest of his self-preservation. To do so means to defend his right to life, liberty, and estate (*Second Treatise*, II.6; see Polin 1967, 20). To renounce these rights—man's *natural rights*—would be a violation of the law of nature. Man is obligated by virtue of being a man to observe these natural rights. Locke states that by "violating the law [of nature], and varying from the right rule of reason . . . a man so far becomes degenerate, and declares himself to quit the principles of human nature, and to be a noxious creature" (*Second Treatise*, II.10). If a man does forfeit his right to freedom, as in the case of slavery, then he cannot be "considered as any part of *civil society*" (*Second Treatise*, VII.85; emphasis original). The slave is subject to the absolute and arbitrary power of the master but, Locke says, man's "freedom from absolute, arbitrary power is so necessary to, and closely joined with a man's preservation, that he cannot part with it" (*Second Treatise*, IV.23). Thus the additional price paid for the forfeiture of one's natural rights is the forfeiture of one's status as a moral being. The rights that stem from man's observance of natural law, that is *reason*, are inextricable from man's very being. To renounce them is to cease to be a man.

Locke's views on inalienable rights are a source of considerable debate in the scholarly literature. One side of this debate argues that Locke considered *no* rights to be inalienable, but believed that certain rights were simply not possessed by man, remaining, instead, with God. This argument is made by Simmons, who contends that the alienation of *all* our rights would not make us slaves because we do not possess the right to total control over our lives and liberty (1993, 115–16). Simmons suggests that the lack of an explicit theory of inalienable rights in Locke's writing stems from the fact that those rights retained upon entering civil society (rights necessary to self-preservation, which might be considered inalienable), were simply not owned by man. Locke viewed all of man's rights to be alienable because man does not possess the right to subject himself to extreme danger or death (Simmons 1992, 232–33; 1993, 102). According to this view, the rights that man enjoys over his life, liberty, and property are *use rights* only and, though they constitute *property*, they are not *possessions*, and man's right to them does not include the right of alienation (*Second Treatise*, II.6, XI.135; see also Tully 1980, 114). Locke argues that, since "nobody has an absolute arbitrary power over himself," then no one can possibly transfer such a right to another (*Second Treatise*, IV.23, XI.135). Simmons's viewpoint interprets Locke's statement that man is *"bound to preserve himself,* and not quit his station willfully," as man's right and duty as a servant of God (*Second Treatise*, II.6; emphasis original). Man is not endowed with the ability to give this right away. That we have property in our person means that we are free to exercise some control over our lives, liberty, and estate, but not insofar as might put our preservation in jeopardy.

Glenn, on the contrary, argues that Locke *does* have a theory of inalienable rights and that it is in his prohibition of suicide (i.e., the inalienability of the right to self-preservation) that it may be most clearly seen. Looking at paragraph six of the *Second Treatise*, which states that man has "not liberty to destroy himself" and is *"bound to preserve himself,"* Glenn sees an inalienable right where Simmons sees a right not possessed. Glenn argues that the inalienability of man's right to self-preservation does not rest solely—in fact need not rest at all—on his being the workmanship of God. Reason alone is sufficient to guide man toward the inalienability of certain rights (Glenn 1984, 87). In *John Locke's Liberalism*, Grant sees both lines of argument to be present in Locke's writing. Locke contends that, on the one hand, our property in rights is given to us by God in a qualified manner and may be disposed of only with his permission. On the other hand, to alienate one's right to life or liberty would be to go against reason (Grant 1987, 68–69). Man is doubly guaranteed not to alienate his life, freedom, or property. First, the law of nature (reason) will always steer him from that which puts him in grave danger. Locke, after all, defines the *person* as "a thinking intelligent being, that has *reason and reflection,* and can consider itself as itself" (*Essay*, II.27.11, emphasis added). And, second, should he want (in violation of the law of nature) to relinquish such rights as are necessary to his preservation, he would not be able to because he lacks them to begin with. Whether defended through man's unique ability to reason, or protected by man's relationship with God, the exercise of man's natural right is a crucial and necessary part of his being as a man.

ROUSSEAU

Rousseau picks up the thread of those before him regarding the intimate ties between the inalienable rights of man and that which constitutes a moral being. In *The Social Contract*, Rousseau is explicit regarding the relationship between man's liberty and his being as a man. Taking exception to the idea (in this case, of Grotius) that a man may alienate his freedom, Rousseau calls it "absurd and inconceivable" that men might give themselves to the authority of another without just compensation (and for the renouncement of liberty, no just compensation exists). He states that, "[t]o renounce liberty is to renounce being a man, to surrender the rights of humanity and even its duties . . . Such a renunciation is incomparable with man's nature; to remove all liberty from his will is to remove all morality from his acts" (*SC*, I.4).

Rousseau contends that the alienation of life and freedom to another is not possible because what one alienates becomes separate from its original owner, who no longer has any interest in it. This may be said of property, but it cannot be said of one's life or freedom. One cannot be believed to have no future interest in what becomes of his life and liberty, and there is not adequate compensation for the loss of either. To relinquish these rights would, "offend both nature and reason" (*Second Discourse*, 168).

Rousseau contests the belief of Grotius and others that conquest is a legitimate basis for slavery. Rousseau bases his argument on the belief that wars occur between states, not men; therefore, following a victory, the conquered is no longer an enemy and the victor enjoys no right over him. "The words *slave* and *right* contradict each other and are mutually exclusive" (*SC*, I.4; emphasis original). Just as Rousseau believes the relationship between slave and master to be illegitimate, so does he believe the relationship between a people and a king to be unjust. Relationships such as these operate only to the advantage of the king, whose interests remain his own (*SC*, I.5). Such associations "destroyed natural freedom for all time, established forever the law of property and inequality, changed a clever usurpation into an irrevocable right, and for the profit of a few ambitious men henceforth subjected the whole human race to work, servitude and misery" (*Second Discourse*, 160).

Rousseau decries any conditions under which a man might give up his freedom to another. It cannot be legitimately surrendered either voluntarily or by force or coercion. Man's freedom is an inherent and, thus, inalienable part of his being.

NOTES

1. Rousseau refers to this work in *The Social Contract*.

2. As Bloom points out, "the establishment of private property is for Locke the beginning of the solution to the political problem while for Rousseau it is the source of the continuing misery of man" (1990, 220).

TWO

The Rousseauian State of Nature

Although Grotius, Hobbes, and Locke differ in their beliefs about what constitutes the "self," they share one assumption: that a "self" has been present in all men at all times. It is in light of this assumption that Rousseau's philosophy of the self is such a departure from those who came before. Rousseau does not accept the self as an original part of man. The self of each individual is the result of social circumstances and interactions. In the presocial state of nature—a time and place devoid of social circumstance and interactions—men had no self. According to Rousseau, man in the state of nature lacked certain characteristics vitally necessary for the development of the self; most importantly, the capacity for reflexive thought. In his *Discourse on the Origin of Inequality Among Men*, Rousseau describes this presocial, prereflective man: one for whom the very existence of the self is prevented by the absence of these elements.

THE NATURAL STATE OF MAN

It is Rousseau's contention that to truly understand man, we must examine him in his natural state. This is *not*, according to Rousseau, the early, semisocial state that many have mistakenly considered to be the state of nature. He contends that, in fact, very little was known about man's natural state because no philosopher had yet examined man's history prior to the establishment of social relationships. Rousseau charges that, "philosophers who have examined the foundations of society have all felt the necessity of going back to the state of nature, but none of them has reached it" (*Second Discourse*, 102). All such philosophers have, according to Rousseau, attributed to natural man mental faculties that he did not possess. "All of them, finally, speaking continually of need, avarice, op-

13

pression, desires, and pride, have carried over to the state of nature ideas they had acquired in society: they spoke about savage man and they described civil man." (*Second Discourse*, 102). Rousseau's natural man is absent these attributes for the simple reason that his mind is not yet capable of such complexities.

The life and mind of Rousseau's savage are characterized by simplicity. Possessing only the most limited and purely physical needs, man in the state of nature is entirely self-sufficient. He suffers from neither his lack of possessions, nor his lack of social relationships. He has no inherent desire to claim anything as *his*. His actions are guided by instinct, for he does not yet possess the ability to reason. The simplicity of the existence of natural man led Rousseau to conclude that, "desiring only the things he knows and knowing only those things the possession of which is in his power or easily acquired, nothing should be so tranquil as his soul and nothing so limited as his mind" (*Second Discourse*, note k, 213). This independent state is made possible by both the plentitude of nature and the simplicity of man's needs. Because nature readily provides the food and shelter that man requires, basic survival demands no mental sophistication, only instinct. As Rousseau writes, "I see him satisfying his hunger under an oak, quenching his thirst at the first stream, finding his bed at the foot of the same tree that furnished his meal; and therewith his needs are satisfied" (*Second Discourse*, 105).

Rousseau differs greatly from his predecessor, Hobbes, regarding the original nature of man. This difference stems largely from the fact that Hobbes attributes to natural man the passions and reasoning of civil man, while Rousseau argues that such attributes arise only as a result of man's individual and social development. Of the natural simplicity of the human mind, Rousseau writes:

> Nothing . . . would have been so miserable as savage man dazzled by enlightenment, tormented by passions, and reasoning about a state different from his own. It was by a very wise providence that his potential faculties were to develop only with the opportunities to exercise them, so that they were neither superfluous and burdensome to him beforehand, nor tardy and useless when needed. He had, in instinct alone, everything necessary for him to live in the state of nature: he has, in a cultivated reason, only what is necessary for him to live in society. (*Second Discourse*, 127–28)

In discussions of the potential for conflict between men in the state of nature, the differing views of Hobbes and Rousseau are clear. Hobbes lists the "three principal causes of quarrel" found in the nature of man as competition, diffidence, and glory (*Leviathan*, XIII, 6). With the exception of the most basic forms of competition, all three causes are necessarily the products of a conscious and reasoning mind. Each of these sentiments has an indisputable social component. They are based on greed, pride, envy, and suspicion, none of which are possible in a preconscious state of nature where men have no real relations with one another. Rousseau, on the other hand, considers the only possible source of conflict in the state of nature to be that basic competition for some physical object (e.g., food) or space (e.g., shelter). Pre-self-conscious man is concerned only with the satisfaction of his physical needs and cares not how others satisfy theirs. Social sentiments are nonexistent. With no society, no relations among men and no true property, the disputes among men can be only superficial and fleeting. It is not until men come together in semipermanent communities that disputes based on right (either real or perceived) are possible.

The independence that Rousseau's natural man enjoys is made possible by the fact that he is perfectly suited to his environs. His abilities correspond to his needs, and his needs are limited to those things readily available to him. Able to meet his needs through instinct and free from the torment of unsatisfied passions, the mind of the savage has no cause to reason. Reason is born of man's struggle to sate his developing passions; therefore, it remains uncultivated in natural man. Only after man has acquired wants beyond his basic needs does his mind begin to develop in an effort to satisfy those appetites:

> It is by [the passions'] activity that our reason is perfected; we seek to know only because we desire to have pleasure; and it is impossible to conceive why one who had neither desires nor fears would go to the trouble of reasoning. The passions in turn derive their origin from our needs, and their progress from our knowledge. For one can desire or fear things only through the ideas one can have of them or by the simple impulsion of nature; and savage man, deprived of any kind of enlightenment, feels only the passion of this last kind. (*Second Discourse*, 115–16)

Passions and reason, not natural to man, remain undeveloped in the state of nature.

NATURAL MAN'S LACK OF SELF-CONSCIOUSNESS

One of the characteristics that allows man to be totally independent in the state of nature is that he lives entirely in the present moment. Unable to comprehend the future, man is unencumbered by the need to prepare for it. Natural man lacks the foresight to make any attempt to claim those things that will satisfy his future needs. He is, in fact, without the knowledge that he will *have* future needs. He knows only that he must provide for himself at a given moment. "His soul, agitated by nothing, is given over to the sole sentiment of its *present* existence without any idea of the future, however near it may be, and his projects, as limited as his views, barely extend to the end of the day" (*Second Discourse*, 117; emphasis added). Rousseau asserts that, in the state of nature, man has all that he requires for the satisfaction of his basic needs and the preservation of the species. At this moment, "the only goods he knows in the universe are nourishment, a female, and repose; the only evils he fears are pain and hunger. I say pain and not death because an animal will never know what it is to die; and knowledge of death and its terrors is one of the first acquisitions that man has made in moving away from the animal condition" (*Second Discourse*, 116). Man in the state of nature still exists in the "animal condition." He lives not day-to-day, but moment-to-moment.

Another key to the independence enjoyed by natural man is his freedom from the influence of passions. Wanting nothing beyond what he can readily provide for himself (i.e., what nature provides for him) allows him self-sufficiency. Natural man is portrayed by Hobbes as a man already plagued by unsatisfied passions and conflicted by his natural and social needs. He is a man divided by his needs and his limited ability to satisfy these needs without the assistance of others. Hobbes's list of man's "simple passions" (appetite, desire, love, aversion, hate, joy, and grief) reveals the already sophisticated psyche of his version of natural man (*Leviathan*, VI, 13). Hobbes considered natural man to be capable of a full range of preferences (in the form of appetites and aversions) and emotions. Given these conditions, natural man, like civil man, was subject to conflict (both internal and external) between his needs and his wants as well as between what he wanted but could not easily obtain. With a multitude of passions and preferences, Hobbes's natural man is dependent upon others for the fulfillment of his desires.

Rousseau's natural man experiences no such split between body and mind or needs and wants, even within himself. He is an entirely instinct-driven being, unable to reflect or to use his mind as an instrument for seeing or sensing the needs of his body. His needs can only be felt physically; his uncomplicated mind does not create needs for him. He is still far removed from the mind having needs of its own. Natural man is an entirely unified being, one within himself and one with his surroundings. Sensing only the physical, natural man is without a *separate* sense of the world around him. He remains incapable of any sentiment regarding his fellow men or his environment, and thus he is not capable of being alienated on any level.[1]

This naturally limited psychological condition is not only one of innocence, but one of true ignorance. Man's simplicity, his goodness, his lack of a violent or acquisitive nature are all rooted in his total lack of knowledge of a way of life other than his own, as well as a lack of conscious understanding of his own situation. To reflect upon his own circumstances and compare himself to others requires an awareness that natural man lacks entirely.

It is Rousseau's belief that natural man is quite literally not *self*-conscious. The existence of the self is, by definition, contingent upon one's awareness of one's self. One who cannot reflect upon his state can have no thoughts about it. Natural man lives in a state of perpetual ignorance; no knowledge or understanding accumulates. He lacks the ability to reflect upon himself, his *self*. Rousseau considers this nonreflective state to be natural: "[i]f nature destined us to be healthy, I almost dare affirm that the state of reflection is a state contrary to nature and that the man who meditates is a depraved animal" (*Second Discourse*, 110). In the *Preface to Narcissus* he speaks even more strongly: "[man] is born to act and to think, not to reflect. Reflection only makes him unhappy without making him better or wiser: it causes him to regret past benefits and keeps him from enjoying the present" (107). Thus, Rousseau views a lack of reflection not as a detriment but, rather, as a natural and preferable state for man. For Rousseau, reflection is a burden that brings with it the potential for a kind of unhappiness from which man was previously immune.

That the self is not an innate part of man means not only that natural man is without a self, but also that the self evolves during the course of man's history (as an individual and as a species). The self is, therefore, the product of that history. It is both formed and *trans*formed as man's awareness of it develops. This takes place as he moves out of the state of nature and begins to form social relationships. For Rousseau, the self is a function of man's environment and his social relationships, and cannot truly be considered out of (or prior to) this context. It is only as man becomes aware of himself—as an individual and as a member of the human species—that the self begins to evolve.

The development of man's self-consciousness is a critical juncture in his history because all of the developments of civil (and semicivil) society are grounded in man's ability to distinguish himself from others. The emergence of language, property, labor, and love all share the same prerequisite—some level of conscious interaction among humans. Such interaction is not possible prior to man becoming a reflective being. One cannot interact with others until one has developed some sense of one's self.

Despite their lack of psychological awareness, natural men (and women) interact on a physical level, and it is to their benefit that they are able to engage in these brief physical unions without jeopardizing their natural isolation. Natural man's solitude of mind suits his circumstances and serves him well. This ability to maintain his isolation is largely the result of his undeveloped mind, but it is also enabled by the difference between two forms of love. Rousseau describes these forms as follows: "[l]et us begin by distinguishing between the moral and the physical in the sentiment of love. The physical is that general desire which inclines one sex to unite with the other. The moral is that which determines this desire and fixes it exclusively on a single object, or which at least gives it a greater degree of energy for this preferred object" (*Second Discourse*, 134). Natural man is incapable of moral love because he is incapable of reflection. This lack of reflection keeps him in a socially isolated state. He is without the mental sophistication to discern one being from another, even from himself. Unable to discriminate, he is certainly unable to feel a preference. His choice of a partner can be based on nothing but convenience and these couplings have no chance of leading to the formation of relationships. Social relationships cannot form until one is capable of recognizing others as similar and yet as individually distinct. According to Rousseau, "[moral love], founded on certain notions of merit and beauty that a savage is not capable of having, and on comparisons he is not capable of making, must be almost null for him" (*Second Discourse*, 134–35). Man must first become aware that he and others share their humanness. Only then will he be capable of recognizing the differences between his fellow men; a necessary prerequisite to the forming of preferences.

SELF-LOVE AND PRIDE

Despite his lack of self-consciousness, natural man does know a form of self-love. This self-love is less a feeling than it is an instinct. Natural man will always act toward his own protection and survival. He values himself in the way that all animals put their own survival above all else. Natural man is not combative, but he will fight in defense of his life. Rousseau speaks at some length of the difference between this natural self-love (*amour de soi*), present in all humans, and a more prideful form of self-love (*amour-propre*), which is seen only in civil man:

> Love of oneself is a natural sentiment which inclines every animal to watch over its own preservation, and which, directed in man by reason and modified by pity, produces humanity and virtue. Vanity is only a relative sentiment, artificial and born in society, which inclines each individual to have greater esteem for himself than for anyone else, inspires in men all the harm they do to one another, and is the true source of honor. This being well understood, I say that in our primitive state, in the true state of nature, vanity does not exist; for each particular man regarding himself as the sole spectator to observe him, as the sole being in the universe to take an interest in him, as the sole judge of his own merit, it is not possible that a sentiment having its source in the comparisons he is not capable of making could spring up in his soul. (*Second Discourse*, note o, 222)

Though he has no conscious thought of being better or more important than those around him (be they human or nonhuman), natural man possesses the instinct to protect his physical being.

It is not until man's consciousness develops and he begins to relate himself to his fellow men that feelings of pride and vanity grow out of his natural love of self. Even then, Rousseau does not consider pride to be necessarily corrupting. It is social interaction that causes pride to emerge, and corrupt society that gives it a corrupting influence on man:

> The sole passion natural to man is *amour de soi* or *amour-propre* taken in the extended sense. This *amoure-propre* in itself or relative to us is good and useful; and since it has no necessary relation to others, it is in this respect naturally neutral. It becomes good or bad only by the application made of it and the relations given to it. Therefore, up to the time when the guide of *amour-propre*, which is reason, can be born, it is important for a child to do nothing because he is seen or heard—nothing, in a word, in relation to others; he must respond only to what nature asks of him, and then he will do nothing but good. (*Emile*, 92; emphasis original)

As man's awareness of himself leads to feelings of pride and right, it is these feelings that lead to the necessity of replacing instinct and pity with laws and mores. Of savage man's emerging awareness of self and relations to others, Rousseau writes, "[a]s soon as men had begun to appreciate one another, and the idea of consideration was formed in their minds, each one claimed a right to it, and it was no longer possible to be disrespectful toward anyone with impunity " (*Second Discourse*, 149).

Early in the discourse, Rousseau describes his subject matter as "[t]o indicate in the progress of things the moment when, right taking the place of violence, nature was subjected to law" (*Second Discourse*, 102). As long as men are preconscious, right cannot supplant violence. The violence that occurs among preconscious men is a tool for resolving their simple (and, according to Rousseau, infrequent) clashes. When, on occasion, two men want the same shelter or the same piece of fruit this dispute may be solved through violence, but the injury is not accompanied by insult because neither feels a right of ownership or a sense of injustice. Losing a contest only leads to indignation when one senses unfairness, and *fairness* is dependent upon *right*. The emergence of man's sense of having rights appears to have occurred when man developed a sense of self and, with that, a sense of pride. Having discovered the characteristics that he shared with his fellows, and having developed the ability to compare himself to them, man began to view himself and others in a new context. "Thus the first glance he directed upon himself produced in him the first stirring of pride; thus, as yet scarcely knowing how to distinguish ranks, and considering himself in the first rank as a species, he prepared himself from afar to claim first rank as an individual" (*Second Discourse*, 144). At this point in his history, man begins the evolution from a savage, nonreflective being to a civil and self-conscious one. Able to see himself for the first time, man is becoming capable of two critical considerations. First, he can look upon himself and, thus, appreciate his strengths and abilities. Second, he can look upon himself *and others*, allowing him to make comparisons. The natural self-love that previously expressed itself only as self-preservation now begins to express itself as a preference for oneself and one's abilities. Comparisons begin to give birth to pride. The natural inclination to protect one's physical self expands to include the protection of one's position and one's rights.

Additionally, now able to truly *see* himself and others, man becomes aware of how he is *seen by* others. Man could not feel wronged by others until he felt entitled to freedom from such wrongs. Now, however, "it was no longer possible to be disrespectful toward anyone with impunity. From this came the first duties of civility, even among savages; and from this any voluntary wrong became an outrage, because along with the harm that resulted from the injury, the offended man saw in it contempt for his person which was often more unbearable than the harm itself" (*Second Discourse*, 149). It was, therefore, the development of self-consciousness and, consequently, of self-respect that resulted in the need for laws. Theft was no longer merely a loss of property (loosely defined), it was now an injustice against one's *self*. Although many events and developments may have contributed to the decay of man and his journey away from the state of nature, it is man's awareness of himself that makes all these events possible. It was not until man gained self-awareness that he was capable of self-alienation, and once he was self-aware, his alienation was inevitable.

THE SOCIAL ISOLATION OF NATURAL MAN

The simple savage is unencumbered by either property or relationships and, just as he does not suffer from his lack of possessions, he is not handicapped by his lack of contact with others. He is, rather, free from "those brusque and continual changes caused by the passions and inconstancy of united peoples" (*Second Discourse*, 107). He not only lacks dependence on others, for, "'what can be the chains of dependence among men who possess nothing?' he knows no benefit from the establishment of human relationships" (*Second Discourse*, 139). Reflecting upon the life of the savage, Rousseau states that he was, "without war and without liaisons, with no need for his fellowmen, likewise with no desire to harm them, perhaps never even recognizing anyone individually" (*Second Discourse*, 137). He lacks even the knowledge that he is a member of the human species, and that this is a trait that he shares with others. Man in the state of nature has no awareness of himself—no self-consciousness. He does not recognize himself and others as members of the same species—alike, but different. Each person is, to him, as independent and different from him as if they were each of a different breed (see *Essay on the Origin of Languages*, 9.1, 9.4).

Man in the state of nature exists as a perfectly whole being on two levels. First, he is *a* whole, rather than a part. Being totally independent and self-sufficient, man is complete. He does not need and is not improved by the existence or the assistance of those around him. Second, man is whole because he is not divided. He is only a man, without the conflict of also needing to be a citizen. His individual needs are his only needs and he is neither obligated to nor capable of considering the needs of others. In *Emile*, Rousseau writes, "Natural man is entirely for himself. He is numerical unity, the absolute whole which is relative only to itself or its kind. Civil man is a fractional unity dependent on the denominator, his value is determined by his relation to the whole, which is the social body" (39–40). One whose value is determined by his relation to the social body is necessarily a conscious, interactive being. His value *is determined*. It is not inherent in his very being. Furthermore, as a member of the social body he must, in turn, be partially responsible for determining the value of others. These civil men must be capable of seeing and judging and comparing their fellows in order to determine their worth. Natural man, on the other hand, has a natural, whole value that is relevant only to him. His value is simply his being. No awareness of self or of others—no interaction at all—is necessary for him to have value; he is wholly self-contained. There is nothing he needs for which he must look outside himself.

It is man's lack of self-awareness that allows him to remain isolated, and it is his isolation that allows him to remain whole. Human relationships would provide no benefit to man, as he is able to fulfill all his needs independently. Extending beyond man's physical independence is the psychological independence that he maintains. Lacking a natural social inclination and feeling no need to act in concert with others, savage man seeks no relationship with his fellows. This is true not only of social relationships, but of familial ones as well. Rousseau describes the savage's ability to procreate without the formation of families:

> Males and females united fortuitously, depending on encounter, occasion, and desire, without speech being a very necessary interpreter of the things they had to say to each other; they left each other with the same ease. The mother nursed the children at first for her own need; then, habit having endeared them to her, she nourished them afterward for their need. As soon as they had the strength to seek their food, they did not delay in leaving the mother herself; and as there was practically no other way to find one another again than not to lose sight of each other, they were soon at the point of not even recognizing one another. (*Second Discourse*, 120–21)

What civil man recognizes as extensions of the self—relationships and, particularly, children—were to savage man merely *things* that happened to coexist in his world. In the social setting, the things and people around us—the things and people with which we surround ourselves—are the means by which we define ourselves—our *self*. In the social world, humans describe themselves in largely relative terms: worker, parent, child, spouse. The self is not considered in isolation. It does not exist in a vacuum. Were the savage man to describe himself, how might he do so? He has no framework. There is nothing to which he relates. He is merely *being*. He merely *is*. He is at once a wholly self-contained entity existing in the midst of the world around him with no specified relationship to the whole and, at the same time, he is himself unspecified. Man is an inseparable, undefined part of that structureless whole. He is simply a collection of matter that accounts for an imprecise part of the larger world around him.

Though man's sexual needs require that he periodically engage in physical partnerings with another human being, he does so in the same way that he satisfies his other needs, finding no *particular* female, but merely a *convenient* female. "Everyone peaceably waits for the impulsion of nature, yields to it without choice with more pleasure than frenzy; and the need satisfied, all desire is extinguished" (*Second Discourse*, 135). There is no relationship beyond the brief physical coupling, and man maintains independence from his partner. Sexual desires are as base and purely physical as the need for food. Partners are moved by a "blind inclination, devoid of any sentiment of the heart" and, having satisfied the need, "the two sexes no longer recognized each other" (*Second Discourse*, 142). Man remains as separated, even isolated, from conjugal partners as from any other human with whom he might have a chance passing.

The simplicity of his mind and his lack of self-awareness prevent the savage from developing any relationship beyond that which is strictly physical. There are no friendships, no partnerships, and certainly no familial bonds under these circumstances. It seems doubtful that the connection between copulation and childbirth is even recognized:

> The man has not the least concern nor perhaps the least idea of the consequences of his actions. One goes off in one direction, the other in another, and there is no likelihood that at the end of nine months they have any memory of having known each other: for this kind of memory, by which one individual gives preference to another for the act of procreation, requires . . . more progress or corruption in the human understanding than can be supposed in man in the state of animality in question here. (*Second Discourse*, note l, 219)

Like the animals around them, humans mate for the satisfaction of a physical need and the survival of the species. Their couplings are without an emotional or social component and have no impact on their solitary way of life.

THE ABSENCE OF MORALITY

It is precisely his reliance on instinct that Rousseau credits for man's good nature. Much has been made of Rousseau's contention that man is naturally "good," but it must be understood that this goodness of natural man is one rooted in naïveté, rather than moral choice. Rousseau finds fault in Hobbes's conclusion that, left to their own devices, men will be subject to frequent conflict. Instead, Rousseau concludes just the opposite—that men, ungoverned and lacking knowledge of evil, will be naturally good and peaceful. Hobbes's state of nature is characterized by (the potential for) war simply because there is no power capable of imposing peace. Hobbes considers man to have a natural predisposition toward conflict with his fellow men (resulting, according to Hobbes, from competition, diffidence, and the need for glory). Hobbes states, "[h]ereby it is manifest that during the time men live without a common power to keep them all in awe, they are in that condition which is called war, and such a war as is of every man against every man" (*Leviathan*, XIII, 8).

For Rousseau, natural man's ignorance of virtue and vice simply allows his peaceful nature to guide him. "Thus one could say that savages are not evil precisely because they do not know what it is to be good; for it is neither the growth of enlightenment nor the restraint of law, but the calm of passions and the ignorance of vice which prevent them from doing evil" (*Second Discourse*, 130). Todorov writes that natural man's goodness, "is displayed in a world that is, according to Rousseau, ignorant of the distinction between good and evil, since man still does not have reason at his disposal" (2001, 6). Understanding natural man's preconscious state is crucial to understanding his natural "goodness." Man's lack of self-consciousness and his inability to perceive himself and others as having positions relative to one another, leaves him at peace. Hobbes's natural man is at war until conventional laws of peace are imposed upon him. Rousseau's natural man is at peace until conventional causes for conflict are imposed upon him, creating the need for laws of peace. Hobbes's belief that men are naturally in positions of conflict and ill will toward one another is based upon the belief that these men are self-conscious and passion-driven. They view themselves and their fellows in relative terms, and vigorously seek to improve their own positions. Rousseau denies the very basis for Hobbes's version of the state of nature. The peace that prevails in Rousseau's state of nature is the product of the placid and premoral state of the men that inhabit it.

Man in the state of nature remains a purely physical being, having not yet acquired any moral component. Of the individual, Rousseau writes, "[b]efore the age of reason we do good and bad without knowing it, and there is no morality in our actions" (*Emile*, 67). The actions of a child cannot be condemned or praised for their good or ill intent; a child is merely a creature of instinct. The same is true of natural man. He is mostly good but never virtuous, sometimes bad but never evil. His actions have no moral tone. In *The Social Contract*, Rousseau marks the beginning of civil society as the beginning of man as a moral being. "The passage from the state of nature to the civil state produces a very remarkable change in man, by substituting justice for instinct in his conduct, and giving his actions the morality they had formerly lacked" (*SC*, I.8). According to Rousseau, precivil man is also premoral man, and one cannot, therefore, judge him on the intent of his actions.

Having thus drawn a distinction between the man who is good because it is not his nature to be bad and the man who is good because he feels morally or legally compelled to be so, Rousseau prefers the former. The *naturally* good man will never be malicious. Because his goodness is not an act of reasoned choice, it cannot be corrupted. The good deeds of civil (reasoning) man are, thus, less reliable than those of savage man.

THE ABSENCE OF REFLECTION AND ALIENATION IN THE STATE OF NATURE

All of the social forces that eventually result in man's inner conflict are absent in the state of nature. Savage men do not "perceive" one another. They have no concept of each other as individuals. They have no capacity for comparison; no ability to form preferences. Without this, one cannot conceive of concepts such as "value" or "esteem." Having nothing but fleeting interaction with one another (and even that is infrequent), savage men have neither need nor desire to please one another. Not only is there no cause to hide one's true feelings *from* others, there is no impetus for having feelings *about* others. Natural men encounter other humans much the same way they encounter plants and animals. Instinct guides them in their actions; sentiments are entirely absent.

That man is not alienated in the state of nature is incontrovertible. A being without awareness of self cannot be alienated from that self. Man acts out of instinct and nature and, therefore, cannot act in a way that conflicts with that nature. Not until self-consciousness develops can self-alienation even be possible. Man cannot feel alienation in the state of nature because man is not capable of *feeling* in the psychological sense. Unable to reflect, he is incapable of feeling sentiments and knows only physical sensations. Unable to "see" himself, man is without even a basic concept of himself and his situation (and how it might be improved). He senses only with his body, not yet with his mind. He cannot feel alienated from himself until he can think of himself as a conscious being. He cannot feel any kind of psychological need or discontent until he is aware of the capacities of the mind. He must first recognize that he has a "nature" and that certain things (e.g., a way of life) are in keeping with that nature. He cannot feel discontent until he is aware of what it means to be content. None of this is available to him as long as he is driven only by instinct.

Furthermore, man cannot feel alienated from others until he has enjoyed the emotional companionship of others. The life of man up to this point is characterized by his lack of contact and lack of bonds with others. Each man lives his life, "with no need of his fellow men, likewise with no desire to harm them, perhaps never even recognizing anyone individually" (*Second Discourse*, 137). Sex is merely a "blind inclination, devoid of any sentiment of the heart," and "even the child no longer meant anything to the mother as soon as he could do without her" (*Second Discourse*, 142). There is no emotional or social component to the minimal contact man does experience. And only after experiencing and appreciating a psychological bond with other humans, which comes only after recognition of others as like himself), can man conceive of that relationship as deficient.

Clearly Rousseau considers man in the state of nature to be necessarily content, even happy. The *Second Discourse* is replete with references to man's serene existence: man's soul, "*agitated by nothing,* is given over to the sole sentiment of its present existence" (117, emphasis added). Rousseau ponders, "what type of misery there can be for a free being whose heart is at peace and whose body is healthy?" and, "I ask if anyone has ever heard it said that a savage in freedom even dreamed of complaining about life and killing himself" (*Second Discourse*, 127). Perhaps most simply, he remarks, "[s]avage man, when he has eaten, is at peace with all nature, and the friend of all his fellow men" (*Second Discourse*, note i, 195). The life of savage man is simply not one into which discontentment could intrude. It is a life of ignorant bliss.

When Rousseau reflects upon the circumstances of civil man in the *Discourses* and *Emile*, he finds man's psychological situation to be a sorry one. The social forces of civil society have worked to change man's nature, to create a new social being in the place of the natural one. Man is separated from his true natural self by the inescapable social dynamic. The transformation that social interaction has brought upon man goes beyond the development of the self to its fairly rapid corruption. Man now strives to be admired and respected by others. This leads him to create himself anew for public consumption. He seeks not to offend, leading him to say other than what is truly on his mind. Man dons what Rousseau calls the "false veil of politeness" (*First Discourse*, 6). Man is furthermore confronted with his often conflicting duties to himself and to his community. Now that he is a "citizen," he must reconcile this with being a "man." Natural man and civil man are virtually unrecognizable as the same being.

NOTE

1. The one near-sentiment of which natural man is capable is pity, which Rousseau calls the "sole natural virtue." Rather than a conscious, social emotion, Rousseau considers pity to be an animal instinct, stating that, "it precedes in [man] the use of all reflection; and [is] so natural that even beasts sometimes give perceptible signs of it" (*Second Discourse*, 130).

THREE

The Path to Alienation

In the Second Part of his *Discourse on the Origin and Foundations of Inequality*, Rousseau traces the development of man from an animal-like being in the state of nature to a civil and social being in modern society. As described in the previous chapter, the state of nature is populated by self-sufficient men. Their interactions are scarce and fleeting. They are entirely independent and whole, content with the simple, nomadic life that they lead. Civil society, on the other hand, is populated by men who can no longer survive on their own. They are dependent upon each other and upon the fulfillment of artificial needs. They are no longer natural. They are divided between the beings they once were and the social world in which they now exist. Despite the relative ease and comfort of their lives, made possible by modern convenience and luxury, they are conspicuously lacking in contentment.

For Rousseau, the psychological nature of man is fundamental, and it is his contention that the social conditions of modern civil society are damaging to man's psychological state. The structure of civil society and the nature of social relationships prove severely detrimental to man's psychological well-being. In *The Longing for Total Revolution*, Bernard Yack observes that, "Rousseau was the first to identify the spirit of modern social interaction as the obstacle to individual wholeness and satisfaction" (1992, 38). Although Yack accurately identifies the resultant loss of man's independence as the reason for Rousseau's contempt for modern society, he does not discuss the alienating effects of this loss. The psychological ramifications of modern civil society do not stop at the absence of independence, but go beyond to the presence of division and alienation within man. It would be too simplistic to say that the savage *enjoys* his independence; it is an *inalienable* part of his existence. It is what allows him to be whole. All of the changes forced upon man by the development

27

of civil society are traceable to and predicated on the development of his self-consciousness.

In Rousseau's version of the state of nature there are no families and no tribes; indeed, there is no emotional interaction among men. None of this is possible among natural men for they possess no meaningful awareness of themselves or of others. Their minds are primitive and they are entirely reliant upon instinct. Between the state of nature and the development of civil society there occurs a single, crucial change within man himself upon which all other changes are predicated: the development of self-consciousness. Man's lack of human relationships in the state of nature is rooted not in the fact that he has neither need nor want of such relationships, but more deeply in the fact that he hasn't the capacity for them. Lacking reflection or a sense of self—in fact, lacking a self at all—man is entirely unequipped for social relationships of any kind. It is not until man becomes a conscious and reflective being that his social development can begin. The development of man's self-consciousness allows him to move out of the state of nature and makes possible the social and structural underpinnings of civil society such as reflection and judgment, human relationships, and the division of labor and property.

EMERGING FROM THE STATE OF NATURE

To understand Rousseau's beliefs about the nature of man, both in the state of nature and out of it, we must understand that Rousseau did not consider man's nature to be static. Examining the nature of men in society does not reveal the nature of pre-social men. In fact, Rousseau believed that such an examination leads one to conclude that, "the human race of one age [is not] the human race of another" (*Second Discourse*, 178). Instead, mankind evolved, for good or ill, along with the passage of time and the change of circumstance. Such evolution was not, however, predestined and intrinsic. Rather, man possessed the *potential* for perfectibility, the development of which required, "the chance combination of several foreign causes which might never have occurred and without which man would have remained eternally in his primitive condition" (*Second Discourse*, 140). It is Rousseau's belief that some series of developments, each building on those before, took place and gradually pulled man from this natural state, moving him into a social form of existence. Although Rousseau is vague as to what may have been the impetus for this transition, he is clear about two aspects of it: that is was fortuitous and not part of nature's original plan; and that, once begun, it was unstoppable. Rousseau refers to man's departure from the state of nature as a "fatal accident, which for the common good ought never to have happened" (*Second Discourse*, 151). Though nature held the tools necessary for man's eventual departure, the trigger is pulled by their combination. Rous-

seau's language: "chance combination," "fatal accident," "happy accident," makes it clear that he does not see this evolution as part of nature's
original plan for the human species. What many consider to be man's
most fortunate moment—being brought out of his rather crude natural
existence and set on the path to modernity—Rousseau instead considers
to be man's great *misfortune*.

Rousseau theorizes that the psychological development of man grew
out of an increasing need to conquer natural obstacles to his survival. As
the proliferation of the human race led to man's dispersal across the
earth, men were increasingly faced with natural conditions not conducive
to the simple self-sufficiency of the original state of nature. Man's expo-
sure to new terrains and vegetation, along with periods of drought, harsh
winters, etc., made it occasionally necessary for man to augment his natural abilities. He did so, at first, with the most rudimentary tools. Perhaps
a stick for reaching the fruit on tall trees, or a sharp rock for breaking
through hard ground. It was this fortification of man's natural abilities
that led to the development of the savage man's mind. The use of these
most basic aids gradually led to man's ability to comprehend relations
between things. He used a stick because it reached *higher* than his arm
alone. Working with the stick was *better* than working without it. He
used the rock because it was *sharper* and *harder* than his bare hand. "This
repeated utilization of various beings in relation to himself, and of some
beings in relation to others, must naturally have engendered in man's
mind perceptions of certain relations" (*Second Discourse*, 143). It was these
initial comparisons that "finally produced in [man] some sort of reflection" (*Second Discourse*, 144). Thus, the vague understanding that one
thing or, more importantly, one's self may be seen *in relation to* another
thing put man on the path to self-awareness. Once man was able to make
judgments about the usefulness of a rock or stick, he became increasingly
aware of making such judgments about other, more sophisticated tools
and, finally, about other men, as well. Having grasped the concepts of
stronger and *faster*, man was now able to consider which men were best
endowed with these natural abilities. Recognizing for the first time the
similarities, as well as the natural inequalities, between himself and his
fellow humans, the seeds of both common interest and competition were
planted in man's mind.[1]

Another consequence of the dissemination of the human race was the
increased frequency with which men came into contact with one another.
Where contact with one's fellows had once been infrequent, random, and
generally meaningless, men were now becoming less nomadic and more
likely to spend extended periods of time in close proximity to one another. This change led to repeated contact with the same individuals.
Such regularity of contact created a foundation upon which the nature of
man's encounters with others was greatly altered. Rousseau calls this the
"epoch of the first revolution, which produced the establishment and

differentiation of families" (*Second Discourse*, 146). Possessing both self-awareness and the ability to make comparisons, man was, for the first time, prepared to form human relationships. It was under these conditions that the first families formed. With the creation of families came a more stable and less nomadic way of life. Families resided in crude huts or caves and, where several families lived in close proximity, communities formed. It was now not only commonplace, but true habit for man to encounter those around him and to form some relationship with them. "Men who until this time wandered in the woods, having adopted a more fixed settlement, slowly come together, unite into different bands, and finally form in each country a particular nation, unified by customs and character" (*Second Discourse*, 148). These early human relationships brought about a great change in the psyche of man. Man's sense of "self" and "others," and his newly acquired capacity for reflection and comparison were all greatly transformed by this transition to a social way of living.

THE ROLE OF PREFERENCE

Man's growing awareness of himself and his ability to see and to consider others awakens in him the capacity for emotional ties. Rousseau makes clear the distinction between physical love, "which inclines one sex to unite with the other," and moral love, "which determines this desire and fixes it exclusively on a single object" (*Second Discourse*, 134). Until this moment in human history, men and women had only the capacity for physical love. Lacking reflective awareness of themselves and incapable of making useful comparisons between potential mates, the unions between men and women were fleeting and based solely on matters of convenience. Of savage man's "selection" of a partner, Rousseau writes, "[h]e heeds solely the temperament he received from nature, and not the taste he has not been able to acquire; any woman is good for him" (*Second Discourse*, 135). At this point in time, however, changes in man and his environment had brought him to a point at which he was prepared for the introduction of moral love. The changes in the way man lived—less transient and isolated—provided him with at least semiregular encounters with (or at least sightings of) the same individuals. In addition, the reflective capabilities of man's developing mind enabled him to recognize those whom he had seen before, and to distinguish one from another. Partnering based upon preference and attraction, rather than mere physical proximity, was now possible.

This desire for a particular partner creates for man a new passion. His needs are no longer as simple as they once were. Where man once felt simply the physical desire for a mate, he now feels both a physical and emotional desire for a particular mate. This desire is stronger, more complex, and less easily satisfied. Man's understanding of relationships—his capacity to judge and to prefer—has expanded his world, but it has also complicated it. Savage man had only to meet his bodily needs—to find food, a partner, or shelter with little regard for specifics. Civil man (or, at least, *semicivil* man) finds his desires directed at particular objects. With this narrowing of man's desires comes the potential for envy and jealousy—more passions with which man was previously unfamiliar. He may not be satisfied with simply what meets his needs. He may deem his neighbor's hut or garden to be on a more desirable plot of land. Or perhaps the woman he desires prefers someone other than him. These are conditions with which man has no previous experience. They are not natural passions, but the products of his development. Natural man's world was one of needs that, once satisfied, were forgotten for a time. Social man, who now covets a *particular* meal and a *particular* partner, must devote more thought and energy to these desires. If he gets them, will he be able to get them again? What if he must compete with others for the object of his desire? What were once simply physical needs have developed into complex passions, the satisfaction of which grows to dominate man's time and energy.

Man's capacity for judgment and comparison has enabled him to see the similarities among human beings and, in doing so, it has also allowed him to see the differences. Many of these differences are purely superficial—differences in hair color and facial features, for example. But others are relative. Man is now aware that he finds some people to be more physically attractive than others, that some are stronger, some are faster, and that there are advantages to the superiority of various qualities. In Rousseau's words, "[t]he one who sang or danced the best, the handsomest, the strongest, the most adroit, or the most eloquent became the most highly considered" (*Second Discourse*, 149). This ability to distinguish and to judge allows for men to be perceived as individuals. Men are, for the first time, acquiring an identity. They may seek to influence this identity not only by accentuating the attributes and abilities upon which it is based, but also by influencing the way they are perceived by others.

The critical effect of these new social conditions combined with man's developing psyche was that, "[e]ach one began to look at the others and to want to be looked at himself, and *public esteem had a value*" (*Second Discourse*, 149; emphasis added). The importance of this single point cannot be overemphasized. For Rousseau, this factor—the value of public esteem—is the creator of modern men. This, perhaps even more than self-consciousness itself, is what separates modern man from the happy savage. It is this factor that transformed man from a *self-regarding* to an *other-regarding* being. Neuhouser argues that it is not merely man's awareness of others or that he is judged by others that is problematic, but rather the importance that that judgment comes to hold for him. He writes, "an alienated self contains within itself none, or too little, of the sources of its own being" (2008, 84). Man's own opinion of himself is eclipsed by the opinions others hold of him. There now exist such things as social acceptance and approval, and men actively seek them. Reflection and comparison have brought to man many new considerations far beyond his mere survival. Man's formerly simple self-love, devoted only to self-preservation, has evolved into a conscious preference for himself *over others*. It now resembles self-promotion more than simple self-preservation. As man comes to understand that he has value and that such value can be viewed relative to those around him (how strong he is, how good a hunter, etc.), he then seeks to increase his value. Man has acquired self-awareness and he has realized that, just as he now sees himself, others see him, as well. Furthermore, just as he is able to compare his abilities to those of others, so are his fellows able to make relative judgments about him. Recognizing this, he begins to place value on the view that others hold of him and he seeks to gain their preference. Such thinking pits men against one another. In the pre-social world, it was possible for all men to have food and shelter. In other words, to have their needs met. But in the social world, only one can be the *best*—the *most* esteemed. It is this desire for public admiration that led Rousseau to write, "[f]rom these first preferences were born on the one hand vanity and contempt, on the other shame and envy; and the fermentation caused by these new leavens eventually produces compounds fatal to happiness and innocence" (*Second Discourse*, 149).

It is at this stage that men acquire the notions of right and respect, and this colors all their involvements with one another. Man's awareness of and interest in the opinions of others changes him to the core. Each man believes himself to be uniquely worthy of esteem and respect and cannot be content without it. Man *depends upon* the opinion of others to corroborate his own good opinion of himself. Neuhouser writes that, [t]he problem that gives rise to alienation . . . is that one relies too much on what others think to confirm whatever conception of one's worth one has" (2008, 85). Man soon feels the need for this esteem much as he needs food and shelter. These men, who previously lived in relative isolation, unaware of themselves and of those around them, are now acutely aware of their relationships with others and of how they fit into the emerging social structure. Being valued by others becomes highly important, and energy and effort are devoted to it. Men begin to affect the qualities that they believe are valued by others. It soon becomes "necessary to appear to be other than what one in fact was. To be and to seem to be became two altogether different things; and from this distinction came conspicuous ostentation, deceptive cunning, and all the vices that follow them." (*Second Discourse*, 155). Man steps away from his natural self in order to create a false, public self and, with this division, he becomes weakened and distracted. He becomes, in a word, alienated. He must contend not only with the division between *his* appearance and *his* reality, but he must assume the same of those he meets. He must constantly maintain the facade he has created and, at the same time, be wary of the facades created by others. No relationships are genuine; no one can be trusted. Man's social world revolves around deception. Of the widening gap between natural (inner) man and his civil (outer) counterpart, Starobinski writes, "[t]he gap between appearance and reality marks the triumph of the "factitious," the ever-growing disparity not only between ourselves and the outside world but between ourselves and our own inner nature" (1988, 27). It is precisely this fractionalization that so concerned Rousseau. Man's natural inclination to be only what he is, unaware of appearances, and to deal with others in a frank and disconnected way must be suppressed. Encounters with others now have consequences. Man has become alienated from his natural self and, instead, feels the desires of the false self that has been created by his environment. In this context, Neuhouser describes alienation as, "the state of existing outside oneself (depending on others' opinions for the affirmation of self) to a degree that is detrimental to one's overall well-being" (2008, 85).

Ironically, the social and material things that man strives for in an effort to satisfy his desires only serve to drive him further away from his original nature. Again, according to Starobinski, "[s]ocial man . . . constantly invents new desires, which he cannot satisfy on his own. He needs wealth and prestige. He wants to possess objects and dominate minds. He is truly himself, he believes, only when he enjoys the 'consideration' and respect of others on account of his wealth and appearances" (1988, 27). Man is being pushed further and further from his true self by the false needs and desires that society creates for him. The social recognition and material possessions for which he strives only leave him weaker and more divided. Rousseau makes the depths of man's transformation clear when he states that, "the savage lives within himself; the sociable man, always outside of himself, knows how to live only in the opinion of others; and it is, so to speak, from their judgment alone that he draws *the sentiment of his own existence*" (*Second Discourse*, 179; emphasis added). Sociable man is dependent upon others for the very thing that makes him human. Without others he is without a sense of himself. Perhaps no stronger statement could be made regarding man's dependence on other men. It is as if, were he not defined by the judgment of others, he would cease to exist for himself.

MAN'S DEPENDENCE ON OTHERS

For Rousseau, loss of the absolute self-sufficiency and independence that man enjoyed in the state of nature is perhaps the most serious and detrimental consequence of civil society. In *Emile*, Rousseau states clearly that, "[d]ependence on men, since it is without order, engenders all the vices, and by it, master and slave are mutually corrupted" (85). Only man's dependence on *things* can be seen as natural—all forms of dependence on *other men* is unnatural and inherently corrupting. As Morgenstern has stated, "Rousseau insists that any person who is not self-sufficient—that is, who cannot rely upon himself alone to provide for all his needs and wishes—is inherently powerless" (1996, 142). The only true power that a man may possess is the power that comes with total self-sufficiency. The things that make modern men "powerful," such as social standing or wealth, are dependent upon the social structure. If there is no commerce, wealth has no meaning. If there is no social hierarchy, all men are equal. Independence was the greatest strength that natural man possessed and to render him dependent is to render him weak.

Man's dependence on others is both inherently unnatural and inherently alienating. Man is naturally independent and, when he is made dependent, his original nature is corrupted. Morgenstern argues that, "[t]his consciousness of Self and Other separates Savage Man from Natural Man. Henceforth, Natural Man's existence is no longer undifferentiated: he cannot claim, as Savage Man once did, to be entirely at one with himself. This self-awareness has its effect on every area of Natural Man's life, for it is this consciousness that enables man to alienate himself and his existence" (1996, 135). The natural, whole self and the unnatural, dependent self are *necessarily* alienated from one another. The mere existence of each stands in direct opposition to the other.

There is some disagreement as to whether Rousseau considered man's corruption and alienation to be inevitable consequences of the dependence that comes from his departure from the state of nature. Dent, for example, argues that dependence on others is *not necessarily* problematic: "[w]e can depend on others because we are not economically self-sufficient; or not emotionally sufficient to ourselves; or not capable of sustaining a sense of our own personal worth without endless 'stroking.' . . . To say, as many have done, that Rousseau sees 'dependence' *tout court* as containing the seeds of all our trouble is not to see what he is saying" (1989, 33). Similarly, Grant contends that if we focus on the effects of dependence on integrity, rather than authenticity, we do not find all forms of dependence to be corrupting. She holds out as examples of non-corrupting dependence that of children on parents and the mutual dependence of friends or lovers (1997, 162–63). But the recognition that there are many forms of dependence on others does not change the fact that *no* form of dependence on other men existed in the state of nature (even the bond of dependence of the child on its mother was brief); therefore *all* forms of dependence represent a departure from man's natural state. Thus, while some forms of dependence may not corrupt man's moral integrity, they nonetheless corrupt man's naturally independent state. Furthermore, while we might not expect the mutual dependence of friends to be detrimental, any form of dependence creates a vulnerability that did not exist in man's natural state.

It is true that Rousseau speaks of the great joy man gets from his conjugal and paternal relationships. But it is out of the familial bond that is born the division of labor, and several families together create the first community. It is a slippery slope in the direction of corrupt society. It is not a question of whether or not all of the developments beyond the state of nature are corrupting, but rather whether the "good" developments can occur without *necessarily* leading to the corrupting ones. I believe Rousseau's answer here is "no." Can man take a partner without allowing this partnership to usurp his self-sufficiency? Can men live with others in a community and not engage in some division of labor, leading them to depend upon one another? Can man enjoy self-awareness and reflection without using these faculties to make judgments about others? Can he witness the respect and adoration that some receive and not actively seek it for himself? Under modern social circumstances, he cannot. The self-consciousness that makes man's personal and social development possible, likewise, makes his corruption inevitable.

THE DIVISION OF LABOR

Just as civil society subjects man to an unnatural psychological need for his fellows, so, too, does it create unnatural tangible needs. The division of labor that grows out of the creation of communities makes life more comfortable for man, but it solidifies the need for the existence and cooperation of others. Although the division of labor is formalized by the invention of metallurgy and agriculture, its origin predates them. The first families lead to "the first difference . . . in the way of life of the two sexes. . . . Women became more sedentary and grew accustomed to tend the hut and the children, while the man went to seek their common subsistence" (*Second Discourse*, 147). These simple changes in the lives of men and women are sufficient to cause them to become softened by their somewhat easier life. Extending from this, the community as a whole then discovers the pleasure of leisure and of the possession of "things." It is, in Rousseau's words:

> The first yoke they imposed on themselves without thinking about it, and the first source of evils they prepared for their descendants. For, besides their continuing thus to soften body and mind, as these commodities had lost almost all their pleasantness through habit, and as they had at the same time degenerated into true needs, being deprived of them became much more cruel than possessing them was sweet; and people were unhappy to lose them without being happy to possess them. (*Second Discourse*, 147)

This particular type of dependence on things goes beyond the natural dependence on food, shelter, and the like. Man has created dependence for himself, needing things that are not required for him to live, but only for him to live more comfortably.

The division of labor serves to drive man further away from his natural self by exacerbating his dependence on others. Though the division of labor is not responsible for man's need for others, it introduces him to new ways of being dependent—to new things to need others *for*. It further separates man from his natural, solitary existence and it fosters both a need for others and a need for things. Man now has needs that exceed his grasp, and he longs for things whose value or function would have been a mystery to him in the state of nature. He has been robbed of the natural freedom that he enjoyed as a self-sufficient being guided only by nature (*Emile*, 84–85; see Miller 1984, 173). The creature comforts that man learned to enjoy soon developed into necessities as he became not only unwilling but also unable to provide for himself as he once had. Rousseau observes man, "having formerly been free and independent . . . due to a multitude of new needs, subjected so to speak to all of nature and especially to his fellow men, whose slave he becomes in a sense even in becoming their master; rich, he needs their services; poor, he needs their help; and mediocrity cannot enable him to do without them" (*Second Discourse*, 156). Man's interest in others becomes limited to only how he can be best served, until finally, "the fervor to raise one's relative fortune less out of true need than in order to place oneself above others, inspires in men a base inclination to harm others" (*Second Discourse*, 156). From man's ability to recognize his fellows and to compare himself to them has grown an all consuming need to surpass them. Soon after acquiring the ability to compare himself to others, man began to feel the impulsion to find himself (and be found by others) superior to them.

Rousseau considers the division of labor to alienate man from the source of his existence in much the same way that Marx later considers the creation of wage labor to alienate man from the product of his labor. Asher Horowitz discusses the alienating effects of the division of labor as described by Rousseau in the *Second Discourse*, but by stressing the economic aspect of (Rousseauian) civil society as a cause of man's alienation, Horowitz underestimates the importance of the psychological aspect. Painting Rousseau as a proto-Marxist, Horowitz places heavy emphasis on the role of money in the emergent division of labor, stating that, "[i]n civil society . . . the primary necessity is the necessity for money" (1987, 122). But civil man's need for money is just a symptom of his artificial dependence. Money is perhaps the *most* artificial invention of civil society. It *is* nothing. Its value is entirely created by the society. That man was once entirely self-sufficient and is now dependent upon money serves as a metaphor for man's loss of psychological independence. Man's loss of independence has been complete. There is no aspect of his life in which he is not reliant on others. It is the effects of civil society on the social and psychological facets of man that Rousseau finds most disturbing. In this mutually dependent society, man is enslaved, whatever his status. Master and slave are equally bound, and both are corrupted (*Second Discourse*, 156; *Emile*, 85; Shklar 1978, 15; Melzer 1980, 1020).

THE PROBLEM OF PRIVATE PROPERTY

Rousseau places considerable emphasis on the meaning of private property in civil society. Its establishment is one of the great changes that take place as man moves toward civil society, and it is responsible for many changes in the ways in which men relate to one another. Rousseau begins the Second Part of his *Second Discourse* with the following statement: "[t]he first person who, having fenced off a plot of ground, took it into his head to say *this is mine* and found people simple enough to believe him, was the true founder of civil society" (141; emphasis original). As Bloom has stated, "[Rousseau's] critique of modern economics and his questions about the legitimacy of private property are at the root of socialism, particularly Marxism" (1990, 214). Property figures prominently in both Rousseau's and Marx's critiques of modern society, and yet for each it is representative of different problems. For Marx, private property is the tangible result of alienated labor. He states, "[p]rivate *property* is thus the product, the result, the necessary consequence, of *alienated labour*, of the external relation of the worker to nature and to himself" (*E&PM*, 79; emphasis original). Private property is a manifestation of the economic conditions under which man becomes alienated from his labor. For Marx, it is symbolic of man's alienation.

For Rousseau, property represents man's loss of independence. As with money (a form of property), the role of property in the life of civil man is a reflection of his pervasive dependence on others. In discussing the simple life of man in the state of nature, Rousseau speculates on his freedom with the question, "what can be the chains of dependence among men who possess nothing?" (*Second Discourse*, 139). The need to acquire and maintain property reinforces man's dependence. Furthermore, property becomes the tool by which men are measured and acts as a catalyst for the deterioration of human relationships. Possession of private property is one of the ways that society renders men unequal. There is no natural basis for one man to possess more than another, thus making him more powerful; yet, private property creates such conditions. Of Rousseau's concern with private property, Allan Bloom writes, "Rousseau, followed by Marx, thought that the inner logic of acquisition would concentrate wealth in fewer and fewer hands, completely dispossessing the poor and alienating them from the means of becoming prosperous" (1990, 223). Men come to judge one another by what they possess, and are blindly driven to possess more. This finally results in a state in which "the fervor to raise one's relative fortune less out of true need than in order to place oneself above others, inspires in all men a base inclination to harm each other" (*Second Discourse*, 156). Men care only about being better than their fellows and, in civil society, this means having more. The emphasis on property is a manifestation of man's need to compare himself to others. Property, thus, exacerbates man's dependence on others in two ways. First, it furthers his need to be superior to his fellows by creating a universal and measurable tool by which men can be judged. Second, the possession of property solidifies the need for a division of labor, by which some men may procure wealth.

For Rousseau, property is a source of competition and ill-will among men. For Marx, it is a source (and consequence) of the domination of some (most) men by others. For both, it symbolizes dependence and inequality in human relationships and the alienation of man. Marx focuses on the alienation of man from his labor—a consequence of the division of labor. Rousseau focuses on the alienation of man from his natural self—a consequence of man's dependence on others. In both instances, naturally independent beings have been rendered weak and alienated by an artificial social and economic structure. For both, man's greatest loss is his loss of self.

THE LOSS OF MAN'S NATURAL WHOLENESS

As evidenced by the state of nature, it was intended *by nature* that man live independently. In *Emile*, Rousseau equates man's dependence on others with being put back in a childlike state, where men's freedom is "limited by their weakness" (85). For man to live under such unnatural conditions of dependence deprives him of his natural strength and wholeness. Thus, the consequence of man's existence in this society is a soul divided. He is born to be independent and whole, but he lives in a society that makes him dependent. He is ill-suited for the environment in which he exists and, though he appears outwardly to have adapted to his social setting, he suffers from a constant state of inner conflict. Rousseau describes the effects of civil society on man as follows: "[a]lways in contradiction with himself, always floating between his inclinations and his duties, he will never be either man or citizen. He will be good neither for himself nor for others. He will be one of these men of our days: a Frenchman, an Englishman, a bourgeois. He will be nothing" (*Emile*, 40).

The social environment, with all its trappings, produces a false and shallow community of false and shallow men. They are men out of sync with themselves because, although the lives and pursuits of civil men are radically different from those in the state of nature, man's underlying nature has not changed. Todorov writes, "[m]an has a double and contradictory ideal. Yet he can be happy only as a unity" (2001, 16). Civil society takes the individual out of the state of nature and, by requiring him to be a citizen, deprives him of being a man. Neither wholly man nor wholly citizen, civil (bourgeois) man is fractured and dissonant (see *Emile*, 40–41).

It is man's acquired need for the presence of others and all that this entails that imprisons and divides him. In contemporary vernacular, man finds *validation* in his relationships with others and, subsequently, comes to need this validation and the social setting in which it is provided. Almost immediately upon his discovery of self, man finds himself in a social arrangement in which the self is defined by external factors. Natural man did not "lack" a sense of self; he was incapable of possessing it. Having now developed this sense, it is from this that conscious man should derive the sentiment of his existence. But no sooner is he capable of this, than he is denied it. Furthermore, man finds that he must be concerned with his self for reasons other than personal happiness and fulfillment. He must occupy himself (his "self") with how he is perceived by others. The consequence of this is that the self, which should complete man as a conscious being, is quickly turned against him (both by circumstance and by man himself). That which ought to make him whole becomes the instrument that divides. Given to concerns of appearance and driven by the desire to win the esteem of others, the self is changed into something altogether unnatural. Conscious man is comprised of both natural and unnatural components. Man has been divided into two parts: private/public, affected/natural, internal/external. With this division, man's psyche is weakened. Mere existence becomes psychologically taxing because he must be conscious of how he appears. Man's energy, which was once aimed so directly and effortlessly toward his physical survival, is now divided among the many psychological tasks he must perform. Man is engaged in the constant mental effort of maintaining his created self.

It is not possible for man to separate himself from those elements that make him human and still remain whole. His natural freedom and independence are so central to his being that to be without them would destroy his very nature. There is a psychological wholeness rooted in man's freedom and self-sufficiency that is jeopardized by social relationships. In *Emile*, Rousseau writes, "[n]atural man is entirely for himself. He is numerical unity, the absolute whole which is relative only to itself or its kind. Civil man is a fractional unity dependent on the denominator; his value is determined by his relation to the whole, which is the social body" (39–40). Civil man, in other words, cannot stand apart from the society in which he lives. Out of context, his being is incomplete. He needs the social aspect of his being in order to function, but it is not *truly* a part of him. Without his social affections, civil man cannot function, but with them, he is an artificial composite. Society cannot repair the lack of wholeness from which man now suffers.

Being totally independent and self-sufficient, man is complete. He does not need, and is not improved by, the existence or assistance of those around him. He is only man, without the conflict of also needing to be a functioning member of a social body. His individual needs are his only needs and he is neither obligated to nor capable of considering the needs of others. Civil man's wholeness is sabotaged by his participation in the social community. He becomes a part of the larger whole (the social body) and must fulfill the obligations that this entails. These obligations, in turn, conflict with man's personal needs, thus, dividing his allegiances and his inner self. Melzer has emphasized the importance of wholeness and unity to man's existence: "[w]e must have the same goal—be the same person—in every part of our self, or we cannot be at all" (1980, 1023). Man cannot live fully if he is divided between natural (pre-civil) and unnatural (civil/social) parts; nor would it be possible (and certainly not desirable) for him to live entirely *un*naturally. Yet, man's dependence on others and his emergent need for their approval cause him to live and to think outside of himself.

Melzer goes to some length to point out that unity is *not* merely a negative good. The importance of unity is not to save man from a tortured and divided existence, but to allow him a full and happy one. The divided man, the *bourgeois* that Rousseau describes in *Emile*, may not be an unhappy and tortured soul. He may not even be aware of the lesser quality of his life or the unrealized potential for unity of soul. Civil man possesses what Rousseau calls the "sentiment of existence," but rather than coming naturally from within, it is derived from the judgment of others. Rousseau states, *"render man one and you will make him as happy as he is capable of being"* (*Oeuvres complètes*, vol. 3, 510; Melzer's translation and emphasis). Thus, the *true* sentiment of one's own existence is the positive good to be gained from unity.

Melzer states that "[s]elf love is a hunger for life that seeks a *fullness* of existence" (1980, 1021; emphasis original). And later, "[f]ullness of existence . . . is the positive good of unity, lacking which the bourgeois is 'nothing.' He is not tormented, but he suffers from a failure to live" (1980, 1023). Melzer contends that man's desire for self-preservation is not merely a "bundle of instincts and reflexes" but is, in fact, a "conscious desire" (1980, 1021). Although I agree with Melzer's larger argument that man's desire for self-preservation is a "positive desire for life," I take exception with his use of the word "conscious" to describe early man. Natural man may get a great deal of pleasure from his life (in much the same way that some animals can be observed in a state of happiness or contentment), but he is without any conscious awareness of his situation.

NOTE

1. In *Perfection and Disharmony in the Thought of Jean-Jacques Rousseau*, Marks contends that the development of *amour-propre* must be the result of man's natural disposition toward forming exclusive preferences and valuing merit and beauty, but I would argue that the psychological changes brought on by the adoption of tools are sufficient, even in a being not disposed to such sentiments. Once the capacity for comparison exists, preferring one woman to another is no more psychologically complex than preferring the rock to the bare hand or the stick to man's unaided reach.

FOUR

Man in Civil Society

In the *Discourse on the Origin and Foundations of Inequality*, Rousseau creates a picture of man in his natural condition and in his natural environment. A solitary and independent being, natural man is clearly far removed from the modern men that Rousseau encounters. The path that has brought man out of the state of nature and into civil society has transformed him, and the social and economic structure of the modern society in which he now lives serves to both sustain and exacerbate this transformation. The modern men of Rousseau's day bear only a vague resemblance to the natural men he depicts in his *Second Discourse*. Civilization and modernization have so greatly influenced humans as to have created an almost entirely new species.

Man's newfound concern with appearance and refinement has led to a society-wide emphasis on civility. Men shroud their true feelings toward one another in a "false veil of politeness" that ushers in a society characterized by insincerity. Idleness and "vain curiosity" lead to the popularization of the sciences and arts. Such pursuits, Rousseau believes, exacerbate man's preoccupation with appearance and opinion and distract him from the more important pursuit of good citizenship. Furthermore, the arbitrary political, social, and economic inequalities upon which societies and governments are built, along with the false and frivolous pursuits of the people, virtually guarantees their demise. The values around which these societies are built—appearance, acquisition, and illegitimate power—are the very values that are alienating to man. No such society can be considered stable, and all will eventually collapse.

FROM NATURE TO MODERNITY

The modern men that populate the cities of Rousseau's time are not simply more organized and more sophisticated versions of the men that once
wandered the natural landscape. They have been changed in heart, mind,
and body. They are as different from the animal-like men that populated
the earth in the state of nature as they are from the other animals that
existed at that time. Only their exterior reflects those natural men. They
are different in how they act, how they think, and how they relate to one
another. In fact, *that* they relate to one another at all is one of the most
significant differences between natural and modern men. Unlike natural
men, modern men have come to recognize and to know one another.
They are capable of building a history with others, and bonds, both familial and social, have formed. Relationships based upon preference and
attraction have replaced fleeting interactions based solely on convenience. Men have lost much of their original independent nature and are
now forced to live a dependent life that requires the presence of others.
Due to man's dependence on others and to the comforts of communal
living, he has become physically weaker and less agile. Relying less upon
his physical attributes for his survival, his body has become less prepared
to serve him in such a way. So great has been the transformation his
species has undergone that modern man would scarcely recognize his
natural counterpart as the being from which he has evolved. This, for
Rousseau, is the tragedy of civilization. The coming together of humans
to form families and villages (and later, cities and nations) has changed
not only how men live, but who they are. It has permanently altered the
human species.

In the previous chapter, I discussed the ways that natural man was
changed due to the development of the self. Man's psychological development, however, was not the only cause of this transformation. External
factors were at work, as well. The development of civil society played a
significant role in the creation of civil man. Although the earliest pre-
societies may have been little more than groupings of men in their original nature living in close proximity, as societies developed they came to
play a great role in the transformation of man. Rousseau recognizes that
these nascent societies provided certain benefits that men enjoyed. Men
found great pleasure in familial living and their daily lives were eased by
the division of labor. Rousseau even refers to this pre-civil period in
man's history as "the happiest and most durable epoch" (*Second Discourse*, 151). Rousseau recognized, however, that even these rudimentary
"societies," as random and unstructured as they must have been, carried
within them the seeds of man's corruption. Though they may have
brought ease and pleasure into man's life, they could not be considered a
true improvement upon his condition. Rousseau speaks of this period

with foreboding, as if it were the last stage of man's development at which he might be truly happy.

Perhaps most dispiriting to Rousseau was his belief that once begun, the development of civil society and with it, the development of man, was irreversible. It was during this period that men began to acquire property, and Rousseau referred to such acquisitions as, "the first yoke [men] imposed on themselves without thinking about it, and the first source of evils they prepared for their descendants" (*Second Discourse*, 147). These "yokes" came not only in the form of material goods and comfort, but also in the form of relationships with their fellow men. The preferences that men began to show to others gave birth to, "on one hand vanity and contempt, on the other shame and envy; and the fermentation caused by these new leavens eventually produced compounds fatal to happiness and innocence" (*Second Discourse*, 149).

Had it been possible for men to live among their fellows and yet remain entirely oblivious to them, this pre-civil state might have been maintained. But that was not possible, as the same awareness of others that caused men to begin living in familial and communal groupings also allowed them to compare and to judge their fellows and to consider how men's lives might affect one another. Rousseau states, "from the moment one man needed the help of another, as soon as they observed that it was useful for a single person to have provisions for two, equality disappeared, property was introduced, labor became necessary; and vast forests were changed into smiling fields which had to be watered with the sweat of men, and in which slavery and misery were soon seen to germinate and grow with the crops" (*Second Discourse*, 151–52). The same development that had allowed men to reach this epoch propelled them out of it. Thus, Rousseau considers society at any level to be fraught with problems and dangerous potential. Though he recognizes in some of the earliest forms of society developments that are beneficial to man, he sees at the same time the inevitable escalation of these developments. Any society, unless somehow restricted, will evolve into one similar to that which Rousseau observed around him. And similarly, men in such a society will evolve into the corrupted, alienated men of Rousseau's day. The corrupted man and the corrupted society developed hand-in-hand, with men governing society and with the norms and expectations of that society aiding in the creation of "civil" man.

CIVILITY AND SINCERITY

In the state of nature, men have virtually no concern for their fellow men except to the degree that one may constitute an immediate obstacle to another's acquisition of some necessity. When men did encounter one another, they were unencumbered by expectations and were, thus, free to "express" themselves in whatever manner they chose. At this point, the range of human emotions was very limited, and feelings of distrust or anger (e.g., over mutual desire for some good) would have been freely acknowledged. In their occasional dealings with one another, natural men were just that—natural. This candor was not the result of any conscious commitment to sincerity, but rather was because men knew no reason (and probably even lacked the ability) to mask their true sentiments. In these early encounters, "men found their security in the ease of seeing through each other, and that advantage . . . spared them many vices" (*First Discourse*, 6). Under these conditions, any discord would be readily apparent and readily dealt with. Each knew with whom he was dealing, and pretense was nonexistent. Any quarrels between men were most likely superficial and short-lived.

Such candid behavior is not considered "appropriate" in civil societies, however, and, as men became increasingly organized and "civilized," their behavior began to be dictated by social expectations rather than genuine sentiment. The mores of civil society mandated that men treat one another with civility. Ironically, men were required to act with respect toward one another at the same time that they were discovering feelings of animosity and suspicion. But this seemed not to matter, as the civility men showed one another need not be genuine. There are no social norms or dictates regarding how men *feel* toward one another, only how they act and how they appear. But the guise of good will toward others, while perhaps making men appear to be more virtuous, is actually mired in vice. According to Rousseau, to "cover one's wickedness with the dangerous cloak of hypocrisy is not to honor virtue at all. It is to insult it by profaning its emblems. It is to add cowardice and deceit to all other vices" (*Observations*, 50). Rousseau considered sincerity to be paramount, and this modern civility was directly at odds with sincerity. Man must be sincere in both action and expression in order to be unified. Hypocrisy is *necessarily* divisive. By requiring man to speak or act in ways that do not reflect his true feelings and, thus, misrepresenting his true feelings to his fellows, the hypocrisy that public civility requires simultaneously alienates man from himself and from others. The self is divided by the chasm between thought and action or expression.

Whereas behavior in the state of nature was governed by men's simplicity and crudeness, behavior in civil society is governed by the social norm of civility. Social standards of behavior have emerged, and men must adhere to these or risk losing the acceptance of others. Rather than revealing their true, uncensored feelings toward one another, civil men are required to act with decorum, creating a "base and deceptive uniformity" of behavior and custom (*First Discourse*, 38). Under such conditions, men display a civility toward one another that is no reflection of genuine interest or appreciation. It is simply the fulfillment of a societal expectation. Rousseau was greatly concerned by the larger ramifications of this seemingly innocuous social norm. Because this civility would not always (and perhaps not often) be heartfelt, to require it was to require men to be disingenuous. Rousseau described this false civility as, "that softness of character and urbanity of morals which make relations among you so amiable and easy; in a word, the semblance of all virtues without the possession of any" (*First Discourse*, 5). Rousseau believed that, rather than improving the nature of men's relationships with one another, this universally amicable exterior only serves to obscure the true nature of relationships. Nonalienating relationships between men are simply not possible when their interaction is rooted in appearance, rather than reality. Men's dealings with one another may be "amiable and easy," but they are also meaningless and without foundation. There is no actual relationship upon which the polite exterior rests. Nothing in society can be trusted, there will be, "[n]o more sincere friendships; no more real esteem; no more well-based confidence. Suspicions, offenses, fears, coldness, reserve, hate, and betrayal will hide constantly under that uniform and false veil of politeness, under that vaunted urbanity which we owe to the enlightenment of our century" (*First Discourse*, 38). If the same courtly exterior is shown to all, then discerning between friends and adversaries will be virtually impossible. One who offers assistance or guidance could be expressing genuine friendship or positioning himself for some future personal gain. One could never be certain of with whom one was dealing, and must therefore always be on guard. In his essay, "Rousseau and the Modern Cult of Sincerity," Melzer writes, "the modern commercial republic, generating sociability from selfishness, necessarily creates a society of smiling enemies, where each individual pretends to care about others precisely because he cares only about himself" (1997, 282). In the interest of self-preservation, every man must suspect that the regard shown him by others is merely a facade and, very possibly, one that obscures an underlying ill-will. "An enemy will not be grossly insulted," Rousseau laments, "but he will be cleverly slandered" (*First Discourse*, 38). This is, of course, far more dangerous and destabilizing to both the individual and society as a whole than if men's differences were openly displayed. In "Rousseau and the Case Against (and for) the Arts," Kelly characterized this pervasive distrust as follows: "[t]he politeness fostered by the arts replaces a state of occasional war based on force with a state of constant war based on fraud" (1997, 22). The occasional dispute between men has been traded for a continuous undercurrent of discord. With any readily discernable differences between friend and foe erased, men must treat all of their fellows as the former, while suspecting them of being the latter. Being constantly suspicious of the motives of others while engaging in the daily struggle to better one's own standing must certainly have created a great deal of insecurity for man.

There is considerable irony surrounding this alienated state in which man now exists. Though he is in closer and more regular contact with others than he has ever been before, man is isolated by the superficial nature of his relationships. There is no shared bond, no intimacy between these men. Man's isolation in the state of nature was merely a consequence of his lack of psychological and social development. Men did not "feel" isolated from their fellows any more than they "felt" isolated from the animals and the trees. All were simply independent beings and objects existing in a particular locale. The isolation of men in civil society, however, is not benign. Men are isolated because they live behind the facade that they have created. The trappings of civilized life, Rousseau argues, "spread garlands of flowers over the iron chains with which men are burdened, stifle in them the sense of that original liberty to which they were born, make them love their slavery, and turn them into what is called civilized peoples" (*First Discourse*, 36). Though they are now capable of relationships with other men and of discerning good intentions from bad, they merely circle each other in a dance of civility, never making genuine contact. With all men shrouded by this "false veil of politeness," they cannot help but remain relative strangers to one another. One's true nature is never shown, and relationships can never go beyond the superficial. These circumstances create a society of solitary and alienated individuals.

Not only does the falseness of social relationships alienate men from one another, but the social requirement that men *be* false alienates them from themselves. Though man is now consumed with concern for himself to the exclusion of all other interests, it is not his *natural* self to which he is attending. The needs that man is working to satisfy are not basic, natural human needs (e.g., food, shelter). They are "needs" he has acquired through civilized living. They may be necessary for a *certain kind* of life, but not for life itself. This is the primary cause of man's alienation from himself. Rather than living in accordance with the natural, unaltered self that man has only recently discovered—one that has few needs and holds no pretense—he is serving the artificial self that modern society has created. This artificial self becomes the vehicle through which man serves and perpetuates the social structure. He has, in effect, become his own slave. Civil man believes that he knows what he needs and what will make him happy, but he has been deceived. Society has bestowed upon him a slew of wants and aspirations, but all of these possessions and achievements serve only the outer, artificial man, and in so doing, they intensify man's internal division. Melzer highlights the impact of the social world on the individual when he writes, "Rousseau is aware that the public world of honor, power, and status seems to us more real and important. But he endeavors with all his force to convince us that this is a deadly illusion: that the public world is an alienation from the true self, that the private world of feelings and intimacies is actually the more real one" (1997, 288–89).

Civil man is sharply divided between the private self that exists within him and the public self that he displays to others. This bifurcation of man is much more, however, than merely a distinction between public and private or external and internal. It is a distinction between what is natural and what is affected—between true and false. If man's behavior does not reflect his beliefs, then his behavior is insincere. The person that appears in the public realm is a pretense.

Because these competing forces in man cannot be equally served, one must be given primacy and the other subjugated. The demands and norms of modern society mean almost certainly that man's natural being will be buried under the more forceful civil being. The subjugation of the natural self may be so complete that the individual is not even aware of his divided state, but it is there, nonetheless. Were man aware of the presence of these two forces—these two selves—he would, no doubt, recognize that self-preservation dictates the elevation of the civil self over the natural self. Of this man/citizen Rousseau writes, "[h]e who in the civil order wants to preserve the primacy of the sentiments of nature does not know what he wants. Always in contradiction with himself, always floating between his inclinations and his duties, he will never be either man or citizen. . . . He will be one of these men of our days: a Frenchman, an Englishman, a bourgeois. He will be nothing" (*Emile*, 40). Civil society makes it impossible for man to survive if he does not subordinate the "sentiments of nature." Yet the enduring presence of these sentiments, however muted, makes it impossible for him to fully commit himself to "citizenship." The good that man is working to serve, at this point, is actually the good of no one. He does nothing to serve his fellows, but neither does he serve himself. The good he serves is that of a chimera. In his introduction to *Emile*, Allan Bloom describes the bourgeois as, "the man who, when dealing with others, thinks only of himself, and on the other hand, in his understanding of himself, thinks only of others" (1979, 5). Man is divided and confused, and all of his efforts do nothing to enrich him or to improve his position. His efforts serve only to bury deeper the true and natural being.

In this atmosphere of deception and suspicion, man believes that it is other men that serve as his adversaries. His true adversary, however, is the society that pits man against man. Appearing to enable men to live a life fulfilled, civil society instead shackles them to one another, denying them the liberty and the natural sentiment to which their species was born. Rather than providing a framework within which men pursue common goals for the good of all, this type of society provides a framework within which men pursue self-serving goals for personal gain. That they are considered members of a "society" at all is fraudulent. They are interdependent, but they lack any social or communal sentiment. As each seeks to further himself at the expense of others, men are more isolated and more disengaged from one another than was even possible in the state of nature. They are continually *pulled toward* and *pushed from* one other by opposing forces. One's fellow men serve as both the vehicle for and the obstacle to achieving success. Though men are very much in need of one another, they are truly alienated from one another. Kautz describes these men as "too dependent to be wholehearted in (natural, selfish) pursuit of private goods, yet too egoistic to be wholehearted in (moral, selfless) devotion to the community" (1997, 250). Unable to devote himself fully to either his own needs or to those of the community, civil man lacks the wholeness that would allow him to *truly* be either man or citizen. He lives the civil life, but remains only for himself. He accommodates civil society, but neither it nor its other inhabitants have won his allegiance. Eager to win the esteem and admiration of others, man is concerned only with acting in such a way that he may gain these rewards. His behavior is dictated not by what he thinks, but by what he wants. This falseness, created and, in fact, encouraged by society, was one of Rousseau's primary concerns. Allan Bloom described the bourgeois as, "a hypocrite, hiding his true purpose under a guise of public-spiritedness. And hence, needing everyone but unwilling to sacrifice to help others reciprocally in their neediness, he is psychologically at war with everyone" (1990, 215). In pursuing the high opinion of others, man must view himself as others do. He must step away from his true self, for what he thinks and feels are no longer relevant to how he will conduct himself. In order to best secure the admiration of his companions he must live, not for himself, but for them. He must live "in the opinion of others." Rousseau states that, "[T]o be something, to be oneself and always one, a man must act as he speaks, and one of his central criticisms of civil society is that it leads to the introduction of pretense" (*Emile*, 40). A society that requires men to subvert their true nature cannot be a "true" society, for it is founded upon myth.

The fractionalization suffered by the inhabitants of Rousseau's modern society appears inescapable because it is not just the individual, but also society itself, that suffers from disunity. Modern civil society is as alienated from *true community* as modern man is from natural man. The structure of modern, bourgeois society fosters man's dependence on others. Everything that is valued in modern society—wealth, property and esteem—man must get from others. Man cannot succeed in modern society on his own; he can only do so with the help of others. And since each has only his own success in mind, this help is not likely to be given voluntarily or without some cost. To make certain that others will assist him in his struggle to succeed, man must either use them or manipulate them. Of course, he, in turn, is being used and manipulated. Each man is both the perpetrator and the victim of these misdeeds. All are masters, yet all are slaves. Man is now, "subjected . . . especially to his fellowmen, whose slave he becomes in a sense even in becoming their master; rich, he needs their services; poor, he needs their help; and mediocrity cannot enable him to do without them. He must therefore incessantly interest them in his fate, and to make them find their own profit, in fact or in appearance, in working for his" (*Second Discourse*, 156). Man's only hope for success is through the use and exploitation of his fellow men.

THE CORRUPTING ROLE OF THE SCIENCES AND ARTS

In observing men and society in his own time, Rousseau finds another, particular societal force working toward the destruction of man's natural self. The popularization of the sciences and arts exacerbates the corruption of man's nature in both direct and indirect ways. Indirectly, the pursuit of such interests diverts man's attention from more important and more noble aims, such as good citizenship. Speaking of "idle men of letters," Rousseau says, "[t]hey smile disdainfully at the old-fashioned words of fatherland and religion, and devote their talents and philosophy to destroying and debasing all that is sacred among men" (*First Discourse*, 50). More gravely, attention to the sciences and arts has a directly corrupting affect on man by replacing the value of virtue with the value of talent. Man's interest in such frivolous subjects is born largely of vanity and it is in order to distinguish himself from his fellows and to impress them with his talents that an ordinary man will pursue knowledge of the sciences and arts.

In the *Preface to Narcissus*, Rousseau explains how it is that the sciences and arts serve as corrupting influences in contemporary society. It is less the sciences and arts themselves, and more the importance that men have begun to place upon them. Not *letters*, per se, but "the taste for letters." According to Rousseau, the taste for letters "cannot be born in this way in a whole nation except from two bad sources which study maintains and increases in its turn, namely *idleness* and *the desire to distinguish oneself*. In a well-constituted State, each citizen has his duties to fulfill; and these important concerns are too dear to him to allow him the leisure to attend to frivolous speculations" (191; emphasis added). The taste for letters is born of what Rousseau considers to be two of the most corrupting forces in modern society: idleness and the desire to distinguish oneself. Idleness has grown out of man's dependence on others. Now that men have conspired to divide their labor, lessening the burden each bears for his own survival, they have increased their leisure time. Doing so has softened their bodies and weakened their minds. The time that men now have to spend as they choose is not devoted to improving oneself or to good citizenship; it is spent on "frivolous speculations."

The desire to distinguish oneself takes men further away from their duties of citizenship. There is little personal glory in being the good citizen, and so men again focus their efforts on the pursuits that they believe might bring them individual recognition. "The taste for letters, philosophy and the fine arts," Rousseau writes, "destroys love of our primary duties and of genuine glory. Once talents have seized the honors due to virtue, everyone wishes to be an agreeable man and no one concerns himself with being a good man. From this is born still this additional inconsistency that men are rewarded only for qualities that do not depend on them: for our talents are born with us, our virtues alone belong to us" (*Preface to Narcissus*, 191). Just as men in the earliest "pre-societies" sought to distinguish themselves and garner the esteem of their fellows, so, too, do these modern men. Such efforts still come at the expense of man's loyalty to his inner nature, but now they carry an added price. Diverting men from their duties as citizens, the "passion to gain distinction" corrupts not only the individual, but the society at large.

As with letters, Rousseau also acknowledges the *value* of science, but is highly critical of the *teaching* of science. Rousseau contends that an interest in science distracts ordinary men from more worthwhile pursuits. "He who will be a bad versifier or a subaltern geometer all his life would perhaps have become a great cloth maker. Those whom nature intended to be her disciples needed no teachers" (*First Discourse*, 62–63). In other words, those with true scientific genius will naturally follow such pursuits, regardless of formal education, encouragement, or praise. Others who are able to study the sciences only because they have been popularized (and likely have no real talent for such pursuits) may be robbing society of the benefits of their talents in other, more mundane areas. There may be no glory in being a great cloth maker, but a great cloth maker is a true benefit to the society he serves. Just as a taste for the arts may deprive society of good and loyal citizens, so may widespread interest in and teaching of the sciences deprive society of talented craftsmen and dedicated laborers.

In responding to criticism of his *First Discourse*, Rousseau makes a statement regarding the corrupting nature of luxury that mirrors his beliefs about the role of the sciences and arts: that the damage is caused not by their mere presence in society, but by the role they have come to play. "It cannot be said that it is an evil in itself to wear lace trimmed cuffs, an embroidered coat, and to carry an enameled box. But it is an evil to attach some importance to such finery, to deem people who have it happy, and to devote time and effort that every man owes to nobler objects to achieving a position in which to acquire similar things" (*Observations*, 49). It is in this way that Rousseau sees luxury as corrupting not only the rich who enjoy it, but also the poor who covet it. The popularization of the sciences and arts has a corrupting effect not only on those who pursue knowledge in these areas, but on all the members of a society that suffers from a dearth of loyal and virtuous citizens.

"Sciences, letters and Arts," Rousseau states, "spread garlands of flowers over the iron chains with which men are burdened, stifle in them the sentiment of that original liberty for which they seemed to have been born, make them love their slavery, and turn them into what is called civilized peoples" (*First Discourse*, 5). In essence, the very pursuit of the sciences, letters, and arts in society constitutes falseness. The sciences and arts serve as veils that shroud the true and enslaving nature of modern civil society. Such pursuits merely distract men from the fact that what they perceive to be a privileged and civilized way of life is really a denial of the natural freedom that mankind once enjoyed.

It is Rousseau's belief that the popularization of scientific and artistic pursuits in his time had a detrimental effect on both the individual and on society as a whole. These "civilizing" influences have led to an emphasis on men's outward appearance and to an attempt to govern the way that men behave toward one another. Men who have no practical use for an understanding of the sciences and arts pursue such knowledge, nonetheless, spurred on by nothing more than "vain curiosity." Such a pursuit is emblematic of a society in which what is honest and meaningful has given way to what is superficial and, perhaps, irrelevant. Rousseau writes, "[v]irtue has fled as their [sciences and arts] light dawned on our horizon" (*First Discourse*, 39). His disdain for his contemporaries is clear when he states, "[a]ncient politicians incessantly talked about morals and virtue, those of our time talk only of business and money" (*First Discourse*, 51). The worthy pursuits of virtue and citizenship have been obliterated by man's preoccupation with appearance and hollow accomplishment.

THE CREATION AND COLLAPSE OF GOVERNMENT

It is Rousseau's contention that the fallacies upon which civil society is built will inevitably lead to its demise. There are no natural distinctions between the powerful and the powerless, and the laws under which men live are strictly of their own invention. Rousseau carefully considers the conditions that lead up to the formation of early governments. Men are intent upon adding to their material possessions and garnering the esteem of others, all in an effort to elevate themselves to a position superior to that of their fellows. Interaction among men is in the form of one man using others in order to better his standing. They are all in need of each other, but care nothing for each other. Relationships are characterized by, "competition and rivalry on one hand, opposition of interest on the other; and always the hidden desire to profit at the expense of others" (*Second Discourse*, 156). By these artificial measures of wealth and esteem, inequality among men has become apparent and its effects are powerful. Rousseau describes the chaos that results from such conditions:

> The destruction of equality was followed by the most frightful disorder; thus the usurpations of the rich, the brigandage of the poor, the

unbridled passion of all, stifling natural pity and the as yet weak voice of justice, made man avaricious, ambitious, and evil. . . . Nascent society gave way to the most horrible state of war: the human race, debased and desolated, no longer able to turn back or renounce the unhappy acquisitions it had made, and working only toward its shame by abusing the faculties that honor it, brought itself to the brink of its ruin. (*Second Discourse*, 157)

The artificial social structure, based only on what one owns and the false face one shows, has brought out in man the evil and ugly characteristics that will allow him to "succeed" in such conditions, and has drowned out his more natural inclinations of pity and justice toward others. Given conditions of such great risk and uncertainty, Rousseau suggests that the first governments were conceived by the rich as a way of controlling the ungoverned masses and, thereby, protecting their own wealth. By offering peace and security in the form of a united community, the wealthy few solidified and legitimized their superiority over the many. Eager to secure for themselves a more stable environment, men believed what they were being told about a new society characterized by justice and peace. In Rousseau's words:

> All ran to meet their chains thinking they secured their freedom, for although they had enough reason to feel the advantages of a political establishment, they did not have enough experience to foresee its dangers. Those most capable of anticipating the abuses were precisely those who counted on profiting from them; and the wise saw the necessity of resolving to sacrifice one part of their freedom for the preservation of the other. . . .
>
> Such was the origin of society and laws, which gave new fetters to the weak and new forces to the rich, destroyed natural freedom for all time, established forever the law of property and inequality, changed a clever usurpation into an irrevocable right, and the profit of a few ambitious men henceforth subjected the whole human race to work, servitude and misery. (*Second Discourse*, 159–60)

Such were the conditions of the newly governed state. And, according to Rousseau, as one body of men unites, so, too, must all others. The individual cannot possibly stand against the wills of the state. These states, however, remained ungoverned with respect to one another. Nothing facilitated cooperation among them, and wars were frequent. The passage of time proved these conditions to be turbulent for man.

Conditions of inequality became more severe and more apparent to men. Those in power formed factions and alliances, and power eventually passed from the hands of those to whom it had been granted into the hands of those who held it by birthright. The gradual deterioration of peace in the state caused the governors to tighten their grip. The people, now accustomed to being ruled and not wanting to lose the comforts of civilized life, allowed more and greater freedoms to be taken from them.

The false distinctions and inequalities imposed upon these men were corrupting to all, both the governors and the governed. "[C]itizens let themselves be oppressed only insofar as they are carried away by blind ambition; and looking more below than above them, domination becomes dearer to them than independence, and they consent to wear chains in order to give them to others in turn" (*Second Discourse*, 173). From these unnatural conditions come unnatural sentiments. "From the extreme inequality of conditions and fortunes, from the diversity of passions and talents, from useless arts, from pernicious arts, from frivolous sciences would come scores of prejudices equally contrary to reason, happiness and virtue" (*Second Discourse*, 176). The conditions created for man by civil society are antithetical to his natural happiness. At every turn, this society imposes arbitrary restrictions on him. Everything about his daily life—whose leadership he must obey and how he acts toward his fellows—is dictated not by legitimate right, but by social convention. There is no natural nor universally agreed upon foundation for the social and political organization. What can be the future of a society built on such illegitimate grounds? This was to be a society built upon the inequalities of men—inequalities based not upon any natural measures, but rather upon the convention of private property. The very foundation of such a society rendered it invalid. Under such conditions, the society will necessarily be weak and almost certainly be temporary.

According to Rousseau, this unstable state of government will eventually deteriorate into despotism. This is "the ultimate stage of inequality" (*Second Discourse*, 177). It is here that the structure imposed on men by government dissolves and, once again, anarchy reigns. Rousseau describes the social and political deterioration:

> Here all individuals become equal again because they are all nothing; and subjects no longer having any law except the will of the master, nor the master any other rule except his passions, the notions of good and principles of justice vanish once again. Here everything is brought back to the sole law of the stronger, and consequently to a new state of nature different from the one with which we began, in that the one was the state of nature in its purity, and this last is the fruit of an excess of corruption. (*Second Discourse*, 177)

And so, men are no longer unified with one another in a social structure, but nor are they unified individuals. The experience of man in this state of government, from its inception to its demise, has altered his nature. He cannot go backward to his original state but, instead, must find a way to move forward toward a new kind of unity.

FIVE

The Paradox of Alienation

Rousseau ends his *Second Discourse* with his description of the complete deterioration of political society, giving the reader little reason for hope. Having made clear to us that, under the conditions that he describes, the corruption of society and the resulting alienation of man are inevitable and irreversible, one must wonder what hope Rousseau can hold. Earlier in the work, however, Rousseau briefly alludes to the tenets that will later form the core principles of his *Social Contract*. In that work, Rousseau lays forth his plan for a political society in which men are not divided or alienated, but instead are unified individuals while at the same time standing unified as a people. Paradoxically, Rousseau's solution is the same as the problem he seeks to solve—alienation.

In the *Social Contract*, Rousseau reveals little about man's nature or about his present condition. He states simply that his inquiry considers men "as they are." Yet this alone is enough to indicate that Rousseau was devising a system mindful of man's imperfections and of the potential pitfalls of bringing men together. We know from Rousseau's earlier writings that the political and social setting holds great dangers for man. Once a solitary and self-sufficient being in the state of nature, civil society, as Rousseau has witnessed it, transforms natural man into a dependent and alienated creature.

In the societies that Rousseau describes in his works, as well as in the ones that he observes firsthand, man is unable to commit himself to being either man or citizen because these objectives oppose one another within his being. In *Emile*, Rousseau makes very clear the effect of these divided interests:

> He who in the civil order wants to preserve the primacy of the sentiments of nature does not know what he wants. Always in contradiction with himself, always floating between his inclinations and his duties,

> he will never be either man or citizen. He will be good for neither
> himself nor for others. He will be one of these men of our days: a
> Frenchman, an Englishman, a bourgeois. He will be nothing. (*Emile*, 40)

Man's inability to dedicate himself to the good either of himself or of his community renders him good for neither. Far beyond being simply an imperfect man and an imperfect citizen, he is neither man *nor* citizen—he is *nothing*. Clearly, the well-being of social man is devastated by this disunity (see Melzer 1980). The good of the man is to serve his simple, natural needs, while the good of the citizen is to serve the community. But in the societies Rousseau speaks of (and which I have described in earlier chapters), to serve the community is to perpetrate a fraud. With its emphasis on civility, modern civil society requires man to be superficial and insincere, thereby making it impossible for him to serve both his individual needs and the needs of the community. Rousseau further describes the plight of social men:

> [s]wept along in contrary routes by nature and by men, forced to divide ourselves between these different impulses, we follow a composite impulse which leads us to neither one goal nor the other. Thus, in conflict and floating during the whole course of our life, we end it without having been able to put ourselves in harmony with ourselves and without having been good either for ourselves or for others. (*Emile*, 41)

To be able to serve both oneself as an individual and the community, yet not be divided and alienated, the *man* and the *citizen* must be merged into one. In order for this to be possible, their respective goods must be merged. Only when what is good for the individual is truly the same as what is good for the community can man dedicate himself to the good of both. As long as they remain separate, man will be forced to choose and he will be divided and alienated by this choice. Todorov describes this man as, "driven to pursue both ways simultaneously and not being able to do so, he is instead condemned to misery" (2001, 17). Man can only be freed from the impossibility of serving two opposing masters by being released from his obligation to one of them or by uniting the two into one.

If the good of the man and the good of the citizen can be unified, then man need never think of himself as one or the other. He becomes a unified being pursuing a unified good. When what is good for one is good for all, man will wish only good for his fellows. The community that creates a universal good for all men and for society as a whole creates a true civility. Healing the disunity of civil society will facilitate the healing of man's disunity and alienation.

RESTORED UNITY THROUGH ALIENATION

In the early parts of the *Social Contract*, Rousseau deals very directly with the concept of alienation. Though this was discussed in chapter 1, it bears revisiting here. Rousseau addresses the works of Grotius, Hobbes, and Locke as they have dealt with the topic of alienation. Rousseau argues against the contention of both Grotius and Hobbes that men can legitimately give themselves over to a ruler. As he has made clear in other writings, Rousseau believes that people are, "born free and equal, [and] alienate their liberty only for their own advantage" (*SC*, I.2). Defining the act of alienating as "to give or to sell," Rousseau strongly argues that there is no logic for men to *give* themselves (their freedom) to a king, and they cannot *sell* themselves because they get nothing in return. Such an apparent relationship would be illegitimate. Rousseau is clear in his statement against the right of man to alienate his liberty to another: "[t]o renounce liberty is to renounce being a man. . . . Such a renunciation is incomparable with man's nature; to remove all liberty from his will is to remove all morality from his acts" (*SC*, I.4). When men allow themselves to be subject to a ruler they do not, in turn, get their livelihood from him. On the contrary, he takes his from them. There is no legitimate basis for such a renunciation. No man can legitimately act in a way that is detrimental to his own interests and his own survival and, since "the force and liberty of each man are the chief instruments of his self-preservation, how can he pledge them without harming his own interests, and neglecting the care he owes himself?" (*SC*, I.6). This is the question that Rousseau takes on in writing *The Social Contract*.

Rousseau clearly has the importance of man's liberty in mind when he states the problem that he is addressing in *The Social Contract*: "to find a form of association which will defend and protect with the whole common force the person and goods of each associate, and in which each, while uniting himself with all, may still obey himself alone, and remain as free as before" (*SC*, I.6). The preservation of man's personal independence is not subordinated to the defense of his person and property. The good society must be able to protect the individual and his property, but it must also protect his personal freedom and his oneness with the community as a whole.

So how is it that, after making this statement that so fervently defends the preservation of man's liberty, Rousseau then calls for each man's "total alienation"? First we must look closely at the surrender that Rousseau describes. Though lengthy, the entire description bears including here:

> the total alienation of each associate, together with all his rights, to the whole community; for, in the first place, as each gives himself absolute-

ly, the conditions are the same for all; and, this being so, no one has any interest in making them burdensome to others.

Moreover, the alienation being without reserve, the union is as perfect as it can be, and no associate has anything more to demand: for, if the individuals retained certain rights, as there would be no common superior to decide between them and the public, each, being on one point his own judge, would ask to be so on all; the state of nature would thus continue, and the association would necessarily become inoperative or tyrannical.

Finally, each man, in giving himself to all, gives himself to nobody; and as there is no associate over which he does not acquire the same right as he yields others over himself, he gains an equivalent for everything he loses, and an increase of force for the preservation of what he has. (*SC*, I.6)

The main points here are two. First, that all men enter the social contract under the same conditions. Giving up all of one's rights, as well as any potential rights one might have over another, no one is ruler and no one is ruled. No one enjoys any rights of governance over others. The positive good of this condition is that all men are equal. The negative good is that such conditions ensure that men will *remain* equal. No man can worsen the conditions for others without also worsening them for himself and, likewise, no man can improve his state without improving that of the entire community. Such conditions eliminate the risk of anyone pursuing individual interests that contradict the interests of the community. As Rousseau states, "it is impossible to offend against one of the members without attacking the body, and still more to offend against the body without the members resenting it" (*SC*, I.7). Though ideally, all citizens would be truly committed to the good of the community, these conditions guard against the "rogue" member of society.

Second, in giving himself to the community as a whole, man gives himself to no individual. Rather than forfeiting his independence to a ruler or a governing body, man gives his liberty over to the amalgamation of all members, himself included. He gives his liberty and his power as an individual over to the very body from which he will get his strength. In this way he is able to alienate his liberty and yet not be left an alienated being. He gets back liberty and power in the same measure as he gives, but what he gets back is not individual liberty or individual power, but rather the liberty and power of the unified, communal whole. No one member has any power over him nor does he enjoy power over his fellows. Instead, they each have power only as a part of the whole and are likewise only subject to the governance of all members acting together as the sovereign. By giving himself over to a body of which he is an equal and active part, man is able to alienate his rights without being psychologically alienated. He is not diminished by the surrender of rights, for he gets back, in another form, all that he has given.

In the second paragraph of the above passage, Rousseau seems to anticipate those who would recoil at his proposal of complete surrender to the community. Rousseau defends his prescription in stating the consequences of "the individuals retaining certain rights." If men retained their rights in certain areas, they would continue to act in their own interest in these areas. Because the aim of the social contract is to unify the individual interest with the communal interest, the retaining of certain rights would be a great detriment. Furthermore, men would continue to be divided beings, as their interests would continue to be divided. The social contract and all its tenets must envelop man. The oneness of the community and man's part in it must touch him in every facet of his life, or he will continue to see himself as a being apart from the whole.

As stated above, the alienation that constitutes the creation of the social contract is legitimate and nonalienating to man because, in return for what he gives to the community, he takes a part of what is given by others. He is not *whole* as he was in the state of nature, but neither is he divided and disunified as he was in previous civil society. Under the social contract, men enjoy a new kind of unity and a new kind of liberty. Rousseau states that "[w]hat every man loses by the social contract is his natural liberty and an unlimited right to everything he tries to get and succeeds in getting; what he gains is civil liberty and the proprietorship of all he possesses." In addition, man acquires, "moral liberty, which alone makes him truly master of himself; for the mere impulse of appetite is slavery, while obedience to a law we prescribe ourselves is liberty" (*SC* I.8). This "obedience to a law we prescribe ourselves," made possible by each man's role as both subject and sovereign, is what frees men from the unnatural inequality and dependence that Rousseau saw in other civil societies.

SUBJECTS AS SOVEREIGN

Men are uniquely obligated to the community under the social contract because they inhabit dual roles. Every man acts as both sovereign and subject. The initial coming together of men under the social contract allows for the spontaneous creation of the sovereign, for the sovereign is the entire community of men acting in concert. "At once, in place of the individual personality of each contracting party, this act of association creates a moral and collective body composed of as many members as the assembly contains voters, and receiving from this act its unity, its common identity, its life, its will" (*SC*, I.6). Thus, immediately prior to the vote that obligates each man to the social contract there exists merely a gathering of men. Immediately after, there exists a *people*, a *state*, a *sovereign*. Because each man becomes both sovereign and subject, he is "bound in a double capacity: as a member of the Sovereign he is bound to the individuals, and as a member of the State he is bound to the Sovereign" (*SC*, I.7).

It is, paradoxically, this dual role as both subject and sovereign that allows man to once again be a unified individual. With the melding of the individual members of society into the communal whole so absolute, the previous social and political distinctions cease to exist. Contrary to the previous models for the alienation of one's liberty to a political community, which Rousseau considered illegitimate, the social contract works because man not only gives, but gets back, as well. In the types of states Rousseau criticizes, men gave rights over to the sovereign and, getting nothing in return, were diminished by this renunciation. Furthermore, because these states were governed by a discrete group of individuals, the interests of the state were likely to be more representative of the interests of the leaders than those of the citizens. This lack of harmony between the state and its citizenry exacerbated the alienation of men. How could one strive to be both the good man and the good citizen when the interests of the individual did not match the interests of the state? Having brought the rulers and the ruled together into one, the social contract unifies the man and the citizen. Man's dual obligation—to the sovereign (of which he is part) as a subject and to the subjects (of which he is one) as part of the sovereign—brings together the interests of the man and the citizen. The interests of each and the interests of all are equally represented by the general will.

ROUSSEAU'S GENERAL WILL

One of the problems often seen with Rousseau's theory of the general will is how it will come to pass that men will put the interests of the community at large before their own interests. The answer is twofold. First, through the work of the legislator men are instilled with a sense of loyalty and community that makes them want to act in ways that will work toward the good of the state. Second, it is not so much required that men put the communal interests *above* their own interests as it is required that they see the interests of the community and their individual interests as coinciding.

The role of the legislator in Rousseau's social contract is a somewhat curious one. He is "the engineer who invents the machine" but, in addition to creating the contract itself, the legislator must also *re*-create the parties to it. Echoing his earlier statement regarding total alienation, Rousseau states that the legislator must "[alter] man's constitution for the purpose of strengthening it" and "take away from man his own resources and give him instead new ones alien to him, and incapable of being made use of without the help of other men" (*SC*, II.7). The legislator is responsible for transforming men from self-interested individuals into communally interested citizens. In Rousseau's words, he must be capable of "changing human nature, of transforming each individual, who is by himself a complete and solitary whole, into part of a greater whole from which he in a manner receives his life and being" (*SC*, II.7). But how is the legislator to convince the man who considers himself already to be whole that he can somehow be made more by becoming a part? The legislator has the difficult task of attracting men to the social contract and persuading them that serving the communal good does not necessitate sacrificing the individual good. In order to instill the unquestioning loyalty to the community necessary for the social contract, Rousseau believes that the legislator must rely on "divine authority" to persuade. When the divine foundation for the community is presented by the great man that is the legislator, Rousseau believes that men will accept the primacy of the community. Perhaps the most important aspect of the general will is that it *comes from* and is *applied to* all men equally. In this regard, it is truly *general*. This perfect equality is critical for the merging of the individual and the communal wills. Rousseau writes,

> Why is it that the general will is always in the right, and that all continuously will the happiness of each one, unless it is because *there is not a man who does not think of "each" as meaning him, and consider himself in voting for all*? This proves that equality of rights and the idea of justice which such equality creates originate in the preference each man gives to himself, and accordingly in the very nature of man. It proves that the general will, to be really such, must be general in its object as well as its essence; that it must both come from all and apply to all. (*SC* II.4, emphasis added)

In other words, knowing that the laws come equally *from* all members of the community and that they will be applied equally *to* all members of the community allows man to consider what is best for himself and what is best for the community at the same time. With the coalescence of the individual and the communal goods, man is able to consider his own good without sacrificing that of the community, and vice versa. He is able to "consider himself in voting for all" and still act in the interest of the general will. There can be no law that will benefit him and not all others, nor can there be any law that will restrict others and not restrict him, as well. The good of each is the good of all, so each man truly wishes for the good of his fellows, which is indistinguishable from his own good and the whole social good. The absolute political and social equality of each member of the social contract means that what is truly good for one is *necessarily* good for all. It would not be accurate to say that men have been persuaded to abandon their self-interest, but rather that men have been persuaded that, under the social contract, self-interest and communal interest concur. Melzer states Rousseau's position as follows: "the general will men have within them is an outgrowth of self-interest, that all citizens have a permanent general will for the simple reason that all have a permanent selfish interest in the common good" (1990, 164).

The general will does not require the relinquishing of individual interests or even, necessarily, the subjugation of individual interests. It simply requires the recognition that, under the social contract, the general will will prevail and, therefore, only those interests that concur with the general will will be served. By inextricably linking the good of the individual to the good of the community, Rousseau turns the idea of self-interest on its head. Assuming self-preservation as one's ultimate goal, one chooses to join the social contract because it offers some measure of security and strength in numbers. Joining in the social contract is an act of self-interest. Once a party to the social contract, however, self-interest becomes virtually indiscernible from communal interest. It is now in one's own interest to act on behalf of the communal interest. If self-preservation is best guaranteed through the preservation of the social contract (and one's participation in it), then self-preservation is dependent upon acting in the communal interest. The communal interest *is* the individual interest.

Rousseau recognizes that men cannot completely dispense of their individual will and that they may continue, at times, to be faced with conflicting inclinations (see Melzer 1980, 1031; Bloom 1990, 225–26). Rousseau resolves this with the following prescription: "that whosoever refuses to obey the general will shall be compelled to do so by the whole body. This means nothing less than that he will be forced to be free; for this is the condition which, by giving each citizen to his country, secures him against all personal dependence" (*SC*, I.7). On the surface, that one could be "forced to be free" seems both an oxymoron and antithetical to the objective of nonalienation. How can one be free and not be alienated if one is forced? The question that must be asked, however, is "forced by whom?" Granted, an individual who refuses to abide by the laws determined by the general will will face certain consequences. But he will not actually be forced to obey the law, only to choose between obedience and punishment. Indeed, the greatest force exerted on the participants to the social contract comes not from the others in the community, but from oneself and from the social contract. [1]

The decision to join the social contract is the first decision one makes in the direction of forcing oneself to be free. The decision to participate in the community guided by the social contract is the decision to accept the freedom that the social contract offers. The very structure of the social contract, which requires that all participate equally in the making of decisions, and that all are affected equally by these decisions, guarantees that the members will be free from dependence and alienation. It is the community itself—the "whole body"—and not the members of the community, that forces all to be free.

The community under the social contract is incapable of honoring the individual will that is not in concert with the general will. As has been stated, man cannot secure any good for himself that will not also be good for all others. Man's knowledge of this fact will, in most cases, be sufficient to allow him to overcome any inclinations not in keeping with the interest of all. Furthermore, man joins the social contract because he seeks the freedom it can provide him. To not obey the contract would be to risk sacrificing that freedom. Only by allowing himself to be entirely dependent upon the community—including allowing himself to be "forced to be free"—can man avoid the dependence on others that characterizes relationships outside of the social contract and that is so alienating to him. Such "force" is the vehicle by which man's unity can be best restored, and the restoration of his unity means the restoration of his soul. As Melzer states, "[t]hrough will, men can forcibly *repress* their inevitable selfish desires in the name of duty or moral obligation. Such moral self-conquest through force of will Rousseau calls 'virtue' or 'moral freedom'" (1980, 1031). Man cannot truly be returned to a *natural* condition of wholeness, but his alienation can be eased under the conditions of community.

UNITY UNDER THE SOCIAL CONTRACT

For Rousseau, the success of the social contract means far more than a functioning political body. Unlike theorists before him, who sought to create a society that would protect man's life and retain some degree of liberty, Rousseau's society must protect life and liberty *and* restore freedom and unity. In a comparison of Rousseau with Hobbes and Locke, Yack states that Rousseau's "[p]olitical institutions must not only secure the conditions in which the individual seeks satisfaction, they must also ennoble his character and heal the wounds of socialization. The legitimate state must produce healthy individuals as well as secure homes" (1992, 69). Societies in which men trade their freedom for physical and material security do little to remedy the alienation of civil (or semi-civil) man. The social contract is designed to heal the individual whose soul has been devastated by the circumstances of modernity. Though man can never be returned to the natural freedom and oneness of the state of nature, he may find a new freedom and peace through community. In *Emile*, Rousseau considers the potential of the political community for restoring man to himself:

> Natural man is entirely for himself. He is numerical unity, the absolute whole which is relative only to itself or its kind. Civil man is a fractional unity dependent on the denominator; his value is determined by his relation to the whole, which is the social body. Good social institutions are those that best know how to denature man, to take his absolute existence from him in order to give him a relative one and transport the *I* into the common unity, with the result that each individual believes

himself no longer one but a part of the unity and no longer feels except within the whole. (*Emile*, 39–40)

Rather than being divided by society, living with others and yet alienated from them, Rousseau's new citizen finds *true* community through the merging of his own interests with those of the community at large. As Melzer argues, "[t]he new self or unity thus produced is a new kind of self. It is no longer a "sensuous" or "natural" self based on what one desires and is, but a "moral" and "ideal" self based on what one wills and respects" (1980, 1031).

Additionally, just as man cannot be truly restored to a natural state of wholeness, neither can he be returned to a state of true independence. The independence that natural man enjoyed was true and complete; he alone was responsible for his existence and he was fully capable of meeting his own needs. Under civil society, men grow dependent upon one another. They are physically dependent upon others for their food and the other goods they need to survive, but more importantly they are also psychologically dependent upon others. The opinion of others becomes man's measure of his worth. Believing that it is the esteem of others that he needs in order to be happy, man cannot find happiness within himself. Nor is he still in command of his thoughts and opinions, for these, too, are now guided by the opinions of others. Under the social contract man lives a life of interdependence very different from either the independence of the state of nature or the dependence of earlier civil society. Men now need each other just to be able to keep the social contract alive. Without each other, there can be no community. Theirs is now an existence that requires the presence and cooperation of others but, rather than a dependence that diminishes the individual, the interdependence of the social contract completes man just as his membership in the community completes the whole of the community. As Melzer states, "disunity is the internalization of our enslavement to what is outside and opposed to us, following from our loss of our primitive self-sufficiency. It is overcome by extending the self to that larger, ordered and self-sufficient whole which includes within it the individual self and all that it depends on. Unity with other men leads to unity within the soul" (1980, 1031). With all men being equally (inter)dependent, each one "gains an equivalent for everything he loses" (*SC*, I.6). There is a perfect balance inherent in the social contract, such that each man can give himself without being diminished and each represents a perfect and equal portion of the whole. Under these circumstances, the need for others is not diminishing and, in fact, the individual is enhanced by his fellowship in the community. Men do not need others for validation or to give their existence meaning. Men do not need to know the thoughts or opinions of others in order to determine their own beliefs or actions. Rousseau's prescription for the determination of the general will demonstrates an element of independence that remains in the lives of these men. Men are not instructed to confer with others or to take a vote in order to arrive at their estimation of the general will. They are instructed to engage in solitary contemplation in order to determine what is best.

The paradox of Rousseau's prescription of dealienation through total alienation appears when one considers the social contract in terms of the individual's political sovereignty but, for Rousseau, this cannot be considered independent of the individual. The paradox falls away when one considers the social contract in terms of the unity of self. Yack writes, "[i]n demanding the alienation of the individual to the community, Rousseau seeks to legitimize and make tolerable the chains of dependence that we must bear in civil society. . . . he demands the complete subordination of the individual *for the sake of the individual*" (1992, 63; emphasis original). Though I disagree that Rousseau calls for the "complete subordination of the individual," the sacrifice that he does call for is indeed for the direct benefit of the individual. The aim of the social contract goes well beyond giving men the security and justice of political and social organization. The aim of the social contract is to create a social organization that returns otherwise alienated men to a state of independence and unity.

Rousseau's attention to man's alienation is significant even beyond the scope of his own writings. His ideas about the importance of man's internal wholeness left a legacy for thinkers such as Hegel and Marx and, though Rousseau never used the term "alienation" in the psychosocial context, his writings certainly prepared its later use in this context. Marx and many after him have sought, like Rousseau, to create a political remedy for man's social and psychological sufferings.

NOTE

1. This takes us back to Rousseau's original task: to devise a community in which man, "while uniting himself with all, may still obey himself alone" (*SC*, 23).

SIX

The Legacy of Rousseau's Innovation

The aim of this book has been to show that, in his writings, Rousseau took the concept of alienation and expanded it from a legal-political notion to one with great significance to psychology and sociology, as well. Rousseau discusses alienation in its traditional, legal-political context in both the *Second Discourse* and *The Social Contract* and, in discussing the legitimacy of political power, he broadens the applicability of inalienability. While agreeing with his predecessors (most notably, Grotius, Hobbes, and Locke) on certain basic inalienable rights (e.g., the right to defend one's self), Rousseau argues much more steadfastly against the alienability of one's freedom than did those who came before. Considering man's freedom to be an inherent part of his nature, Rousseau states that "[t]o renounce liberty is to renounce being a man. . . . Such a renunciation is incomparable with man's nature" (*SC*, I.4). Because a man's freedom is an intrinsic part of what makes him a moral being, to relinquish it would be to deny his very nature.

In the *Second Discourse*, Rousseau delves deeply into the consideration of what is natural to man. He discusses at length the freedom and independence to which man is naturally born. Pre-self-conscious and animal-like in his reliance on instinct, natural man exists free from the burdens and obligations of human relationships. He is entirely free in his actions, guided only by his need to survive. Only when chance circumstances allow consciousness to develop is man's world transformed, and his natural independence begins to wither.

As man's consciousness continues to develop and as he lives in increasingly social conditions, man is moved further and further from what is natural to him and he becomes more and more dependent upon his fellow men. Self-consciousness gives birth to an awareness of others and an understanding of relationships, and man begins to judge others and to consider how he may be judged. The esteem of others becomes important, and man becomes dependent upon others not just for his life of convenience and ease, but for psychological reasons, as well. Under these social conditions, man is alienated both from himself and from others. Man is self-alienated because his life is directed toward the pursuit of external goals. He seeks to be admired by others, rather than to be personally content. Civil man lives life in constant competition for the attention and admiration he craves. Always concerned with how he is viewed by others, man adopts false manners that conceal his true sentiments. He is alienated from his fellows because their relationships are based not on true feeling, but rather on a feigned civility that only serves each man's desire for esteem. Though all relationships give the appearance of being amicable, in reality men are at best, competitors and at worst, enemies. Based upon deceit, these relationships can never be anything but superficial.

It is in *The Social Contract* that Rousseau presents his prescription for transcendence of the alienation from which man suffers. This prescription comes in the form of a paradox. Rousseau calls for the total alienation of man in order to restore him to a condition of unity. By giving himself and all of his rights *to* the community, man is re-unified *by* the community. Though man cannot be returned to a state of *natural* unity, he can enjoy a new kind of *civic* unity. The social contract dictates that all men will participate fully and equally and, in exchange for what they relinquish to the community, each man will receive back from the whole an equal portion of the communal strength. With no man having superior power over any other, men are free from the alienating effects of personal dependence. They are, instead, dependent upon the community as a whole. By reconciling man's individual will with the general will of the entire community, the social contract allows men to overcome the divisive and alienating conflict between man and citizen. The good of man and the good of the citizen are unified; thus man and citizen are unified.

ALIENATION IN ROUSSEAU AND MARX

Rousseau's transformation of alienation into a term with great psychosocial importance is made significant by what use is made of the concept subsequent to his own writings. Few who consider this concept, however, associate it with the works of Rousseau. In fact, the psychosocial conception of alienation is most closely identified not with Rousseau, but with Karl Marx. Though certain affinities between the thought of Rousseau and that of Marx have long been recognized, rarely has more than cursory attention been given to this relationship. Horowitz acknowledges that the parallels between Marx and Rousseau are important, stating that, "[t]here is in Marx's early writings what one recent Kantian reading of the *Social Contract* calls 'an obvious though largely unacknowledged, debt to Rousseau's moral vision of the world, a profound conceptual affinity'" (1987, 5). In elaborating, however, Horowitz focuses more on the economic aspects of Rousseau's thought than on the psychological elements of Marx's theory. Rousseau does address issues relating to economics and private property, but it is from the psychological aspects of Marx's writings that the more important parallels can be drawn.

Marx has been passingly referred to as both "a follower of Rousseau who has been trained by Hegel" (Löwith 1964, 246) and as Rousseau's "spiritual descendent" (Dannhauser 1997, 8), yet Rousseau has never been fully considered as a potential original source of these ideas. In many writings tracing the history of alienation as a psychological and social concept, Rousseau is not even given mention (see Feuer 1962; Edwards 1967; Wiener 1973–1974). Although it is certainly the case that the concept of psycho/social alienation gained widespread recognition and consideration through its treatment in the works of Hegel and Marx, it was quite clearly present as a theme of considerable significance in the works of Rousseau.

The similarities in the conceptualization of alienation by Rousseau and Marx begin in their respective discussions of man in his prealienated condition. For both theorists, the history of man begins with a pre-conscious, animal-like state. Rousseau describes savage man as living a solitary and nomadic life. He has only the most basic physical needs and, lacking foresight, he satisfies those needs only as they arise. His heart and his mind are entirely at peace. He is, "without industry, without speech, without domicile, without war and without liaisons, with no need of his fellowmen, likewise with no desire to harm them" (*Second Discourse*, 137). Man has no sense of himself as an individual or as a member of any species and, instead, accepts that he is simply one element of the whole that is nature.

Marx's view of man in his original state bears a great resemblance to this description. Marx considers man to be melded into nature as an almost seamless part of the larger whole. Man, Marx states, "treats himself as a *universal* and therefore a free being" (*E&PM*, 75; emphasis original). He is free by virtue of his universality. There are no boundaries by which he can be restricted. Marx highlights man's symbiotic relationship with nature by stating that,

> [t]he universality of man is in practice manifested precisely in the universality which makes all nature his *inorganic* body—both inasmuch as nature is (1) his direct means of life, and (2) the material, the object and the instrument of his life-activity. . . . That man's physical and spiritual life is linked to nature means simply that nature is linked to itself, for man is a part of nature." (*E&PM*, 75; emphasis original)

For both Rousseau and Marx, man in his original state is virtually indistinguishable from nature as a whole. As long as man perceives himself to be coterminous with nature, he is not aware of himself as a *species-being*. It is not until man becomes a conscious being that he becomes aware of the fact that he is, in fact, a whole unto himself. This awareness of his separateness from nature is the beginning of man's alienation. Until man can understand that something is not a part of him, he cannot be confronted by it.

Man's awareness of the division between the two sexes plays a significant role in the development of alienation. In Rousseau's state of nature, man will choose any convenient female when he desires sex. It is only when consciousness has developed and man is capable of recognizing individuals and noting their differences that his desire may become fixed on a particular female. This is significant for the development of alienation for two reasons. First, man is capable of preferring a particular female only because he has become a conscious being. Before he was aware of himself as a *man* (part of the human species) and before he was able to make judgments about others, man was incapable of preferring one over another. Once he was able to conceive of certain relationships, however, he found that some things pleased him more than others. This awareness led to the birth of esteem, which had a profound impact on man and on his relationships with others. Man's ability to compare one individual to another, in combination with the fact that men were now living in close proximity to one another (another consequence of the emergence of familial relationships), gave men the opportunity to observe one another and make judgments based upon these observations. As Rousseau states, "[e]ach one began to look at the others and to want to be looked at himself, and public esteem had value. The one who sang or danced the best, the handsomest, the strongest, the most adroit, or the most eloquent became the most highly considered" (*Second Discourse*, 149). Once man came to realize that some were regarded more highly than others, he wanted always to be the one most esteemed. This led him to behave in ways that would please his fellows, with little regard to his natural inclinations. It also led him to adopt the false civility that Rousseau speaks of in the *First Discourse*. In this way, man's ability to prefer one woman over another is an indication of what is to come—his own insatiable need to be esteemed and preferred.

The pairing of particular men with particular women is also important as the first step toward a division of labor. Until men and women began to live together in families, there were no enduring relationships. Now that individuals were sharing homes and meals, however, it made sense to share responsibilities, as well. Both Rousseau and Marx consider the emergence of a division of labor to have had enormous ramifications for the future of man. Gauthier's assessment bears repeating: "[F]or Rousseau, as later for Marx, the primary effect of the division of labor is . . . to enslave [men] by making the exercise of their own capacities dependent on their fellows' alien wills" (2006, 14). For Rousseau, the detriments of the division of labor begin with a weakening of one's physical capacities. With each party now responsible for only some of the duties necessary for survival, "[t]he two sexes began, by their slightly softer life, to lose something of their ferocity and vigor" (*Second Discourse*, 147). By coming together and being jointly responsible, the burden on each individual was lessened somewhat. The lessening of responsibilities led to men becoming physically weaker because they were no longer required to spend the whole of their days in the effort to secure food, etc. Furthermore, the division of labor also marked the advent of leisure time and, as men looked to fill this idle time, new "needs" were created. Rousseau describes this period with great foreboding:

> Since men enjoyed very great leisure, they used it to procure many kinds of commodities unknown to their fathers; and that was the first yoke they imposed on themselves without thinking about it, and the first source of the evils they prepared for their descendants. For, besides their continuing to thus soften the body and mind, as these commodities had lost almost all their pleasantness through habit, and as they had at the same time degenerated into true needs, being deprived of them became much more cruel than possessing them was sweet; and people were unhappy to lose them without being happy to possess them. (*Second Discourse*, 147)

Thus, as a result of the division of labor, men began to acquire, and were never again satisfied with the simple fulfillment of their basic, human needs.

Marx, too, considers the differences between the sexes to be the origin of the division of labor and, although in a way different from Rousseau, an ominous development for man. In describing the first, herd-like gatherings of men, Marx writes, "[T]his sheep-like or tribal consciousness receives its further development and extension through increased productivity, the increase of needs, and, what is fundamental to both of these, the increase of population. With these there develops the division of labour, which was originally the division of labour in the sexual act" (*German Ideology*, 158). For Marx, the division of labor is the precursor to private property, which originates in the family: "the first form [of property] lies in the family, where wife and children are the slaves of the husband. This latent slavery in the family, though still very crude, is the first property, but even at this early state it corresponds perfectly to the definition of modern economists who call it the power of disposing of the labour-power of others" (*German Ideology*, 159–60). The family, then, is the first example of one person's "ownership" of another and of one person's ownership of the labor and product of another. Just as the worker's labor and the product of that labor become the property of the employer, so is the wife's and children's labor and the product of their labor the property of the husband. The oppressive, alienating power structure of modern society originates in the home.

It is in Marx's *Economic and Philosophic Manuscripts of 1844* that he deals most thoroughly with the specific economic causes of man's alienation. Here Marx is addressing the problems that are created for man by wage labor. In premodern, precapitalist society, man labored for his own subsistence. His *life-activity* was directed toward his own well-being and his own survival. Anything that this labor produced (food, clothing, etc.) was for man's own use and, thus, remained connected to him. By contrast, in modern capitalist society the wage laborer labors for the benefit of his employer. Rather than creating a product that will sustain his life, man creates a product that then belongs to his employer in exchange for a wage. Marx considers this exchange structure to be deeply alienating to man. When man's labor and the product of that labor are for some purpose external to man, then a part of man is removed from him.

Both Rousseau and Marx write about the effects of alienation on the very core of man's existence. Rousseau calls this man's "sentiment of existence." Man possesses the sentiment of his existence even before he possesses self-consciousness. It is a *most* basic awareness of his being. For Marx, man's being is synonymous with his "life-activity." It is conscious life-activity that separates humans from other animals. It is when these reflections of man's core being become separated from him—when man gets the sentiment of his existence from others or when his life-activity is directed toward producing on behalf of another—that man becomes alienated.

For Marx, man's *life-activity* is the very essence of his humanness. It is all that he does in the course of living his life. Every species has its own, unique life-activity that reflects the characteristics of that species. Because man's labor (his life-activity) goes into the making of a product, that product is a part of man. But under wage labor conditions the product of man's labor does not stay with him. By being traded to the employer in exchange for a wage, it loses its direct connection to the sustaining of man's life. When man's labor and its product are for some purpose other than sustaining and preserving his own life then, according to Marx, they become alien to man. Marx states that, "the object which labour produces—labour's product—confronts it as *something alien*, as a *power independent* of the producer" (*E&PM*, 71; emphasis original). This "objectification of labour" is deeply at odds with Marx's belief that man's labor is, and should remain, a natural part of man himself. His labor is the workings of his physical being—his life activity. What he puts out in labor, he takes in sustenance. When he labors on behalf of another (wage labor), however, he is separated from the product of his labor. He produces for someone other than himself and what he produces is no longer a part of him, but is alien to him.

The individual in Marx's corrupting economic situation becomes alienated in much the same way that man becomes alienated in the social situations of which Rousseau writes. Though for Marx and Rousseau the central causes may have been different, the resultant problem of alienation was essentially the same. In both instances, man is directed away from the natural and toward some artificial purpose. Whereas natural man acted in order to fulfill a basic, human need, the alienated man acts in order to fill some artificial need. Formerly independent men are made to be dependent upon their fellow men. Marx wrote of the worker, "[h]is labour is . . . not voluntary, but coerced; it is *forced labour*. It is therefore not the satisfaction of a need; it is merely a *means* to satisfy needs external to it" (*E&PM*, 74; emphasis original). Both Rousseau and Marx consider this loss of natural independence to be devastating to man. Though Marx and Rousseau differ on whether or not man is social by nature, both consider the nature of man's relationships with others to be critical. When relations among men are based upon dependence (social dependence for Rousseau, economic dependence for Marx), men become alienated from one another.

Rousseau holds that when man is made to be dependent upon others, he is alienated because he is living an unnatural existence. His purpose is no longer his own well-being and his own survival. Instead, his purpose is now tied to that of others. For Rousseau, social man becomes guided by the whims of society. Always striving to win the esteem of those around him, their pleasure becomes his purpose. At the end of the *Second Discourse*, Rousseau states quite powerfully that the core difference between natural man and civil man is that natural man lives "within himself," while civil man "always outside himself, knows how to live only in the opinion of others" (179). In other words, something that ought to be entirely contained *within* man has been usurped. Man's sense of himself, the "sentiment of his own existence," is no longer an internal sense, but one for which he must look to others. This is, quite clearly, an alienating condition for man. According to Marx, although man's labor and the product of that labor ought rightly to remain entirely with him, the worker is now required to serve the needs of his employer. When man produces for another (for wages), both his labor and the product of that labor are surrendered by him and, thus, become alien to him. "If the product of labour does not belong to the worker, if it confronts him as an alien power, this can only be because it belongs to some *other man than the worker* (*E&PM*, 78; emphasis original). Having given over the product of his labor (and, in giving the product, man essentially gives his labor—his life-activity), man is now dependent on that *other man* for what he requires—a wage. The other man—the *bourgeois*, in Marx's terminology—is also dependent, for he needs the worker to produce. Marx states that, "[i]n bourgeois society capital is independent and has individuality, while the living person is dependent and has no individuality" (*MCP*,

483). No one is free; neither the bourgeois nor the worker. As Rousseau states in the *Second Discourse*, the master is no freer than the slave.

Though Rousseau made only limited use of the term *bourgeois* in his works, it has come to represent the alienated men that he described. In his chapter titled "The Problem of Bourgeois Society," Löwith begins, "Rousseau's writings contain the first and clearest statement of the human problem of bourgeois society. It consists in the fact that man, in bourgeois society, is not a unified whole. . . . Ever since Rousseau, the incongruity between [man and citizen] has been a fundamental problem of all modern theories of the state and society" (1964, 235). In discussing the alienated state of man in civil society, Rousseau was the first to use the term *bourgeois* in a pejorative sense. He used this term to describe those "modern" men who were neither fully men nor fully citizens. In a well-known passage from *Emile*, Rousseau equates being bourgeois with being *nothing*. In reference to this passage, Bloom writes, "Rousseau is the first writer to use the word *bourgeois* in the modern sense popularized by Marx. It is defined in opposition to *citizen*, and the understanding connected with the term is central to all later political thought" (*Emile*, note 6, 482; emphasis original). Marx relies heavily on the term *bourgeois* in his early writings, and the term remains closely associated with the works of both writers.

Of course, the similarities of Rousseau and Marx on this issue must be viewed through the lens of one very stark difference between the two—the sociability of natural man. It is society itself that is problematic for Rousseau's naturally asocial man, but only wage-labor society is corrupting for Marx's naturally social being. Social living requires too much of Rousseau's alienated man. All human interaction requires pretense and calculation. He must live as a character he has created. Conversely, the social existence of Marx's alienated man is truncated. For Marx, human relationships are crucial to man's happiness, but under capitalism these relationships are characterized by either competition (with his fellow workers) or oppression (by the bourgeois). This deprives man of a genuine bond with others. He lives as a mere cog in the machinery. This difference lends itself to the differing characters of Rousseau's and Marx's remedies. Revolution would not restore well-being or independence to Rousseau's alienated and dependent man. He argues that a corrupted society cannot be uncorrupted, and so his solution requires "men being taken as they are and laws as they might be" (*SC*, 13). Social man cannot be re-made asocial. Perhaps Gauthier puts it best: "[a]*idez-moi* cannot be unsaid" (2006, 44). Rousseau's remedy, therefore, must take conscious and *self*-conscious men and create synergy between the well-being of the individual and the well-being of the community as a whole. *This* is the social contract. For Marx, the undoing of the capitalist economic structure and its replacement with communal living is sufficient to allow naturally social men to live in harmony with others. Transformation of the economic underpinnings (the "base") will lead to transformation of the social and political order (the "superstructure"), which will lead to transformation of the consciousness of men—the end of alienation.

Marx's discussion of alienation is heavily dependent upon the transformation undertaken by Rousseau. He, like Rousseau, looks at the society around him and sees men living unnatural lives, torn apart from their own nature as humans and torn apart from their fellows by the unnatural economic and social conditions. Though Marx does not adopt Rousseau's prescription for unification through total alienation, the core objective of communist society is markedly similar to that of Rousseau's social contract. Through the dissolution of class differences (ending social and economic inequality) and the coming together of men in a unified society, men will overcome both their self-estrangement and their estrangement from others. Their natural freedom and independence will be restored by a society that renders them all equal. Communist society will mean that, "[i]n place of the old bourgeois society, with its classes and class antagonisms, we shall have an association, in which the free development of each is the condition for the free development of all" (*MCP*, 491). As under Rousseau's social contract, the communist society will unify the good of each and the good of all and man will no longer be alienated and disunified by artificial dependence and inequality.

Though volumes have been written about Rousseau and the impact of his work on both political and social theory, his contribution regarding the concept of alienation and the debt owed him by Marx have been largely overlooked. Prior to Rousseau, alienation was considered only in the relatively narrow legal and political sense. As Rousseau himself states in *The Social Contract*, "[t]o alienate is to give or to sell" (*SC*, I.4). He takes this narrow definition and broadens it dramatically through his depiction of modern man as an estranged and internally divided being. Rousseau's work greatly expands the understanding of those things from which man could not be legitimately separated.

In addition to this important innovation, Rousseau further transforms the concept of alienation by holding it up as the solution to the very problem it creates. Only through *total alienation* is man capable of transcending the alienating effects of civil society. Rousseau's treatment of the theme of alienation has had a profound impact on subsequent thought regarding the psychological and social conditions of man, and it is an important part of his work. In his essay "Rousseau and Social Alienation," Bronislaw Baczko writes:

> The Hegelian and Marxist term [alienation] corresponds completely to one of the principal themes of Rousseau's philosophy. To be sure, it is not a matter of seeing Jean-Jacques as a Hegelian or a Marxist before the fact or of reducing his entire corpus to a single theme. However, it

may well be that the attempt to conceptualize Rousseau's social philosophy through critical reflection on the phenomenon of alienation will
highlight one of the fundamental historical functions of Jean-Jacques'
work. (1962, 223)

Though the contributions of Hegel and Marx regarding the concept of
alienation should not be discounted, the important and innovative contributions of Rousseau must be duly recognized and appreciated.

Abbreviations

Essay: *An Essay Concerning Human Understanding*. Vol. I. John Locke.

E&PM: *Economic and Philosophic Manuscripts of 1844*. Karl Marx. In *The Marx-Engels Reader*.

First Discourse: *Discourse on the Sciences and Arts*. Jean-Jacques Rousseau. In *The First and Second Discourses*.

First Treatise: *First Treatise of Government*. John Locke. In *Two Treatises of Civil Government*.

JofH: *The Jurisprudence of Holland*. Hugo Grotius.

MCP: *Manifesto of the Communist Party*. Karl Marx. In *The Marx-Engels Reader*.

Observations: *Observations*(to Stanislaus, King of Poland). Jean-Jacques Rousseau. In *Discourses on the Sciences and Arts and Polemics*.

SC: *The Social Contract*. Jean-Jacques Rousseau.

Second Discourse: *Discourse on the Origin and Foundations of Inequality*. Jean-Jacques Rousseau. In *The First and Second Discourses*.

Second Treatise: *Second Treatise of Government*. John Locke.

W&P: *The Rights of War and Peace*. Hugo Grotius.

Full citations of these works are contained in the bibliography.

Bibliography

Alford, C. Fred. *The Self in Social Theory*. New Haven: Yale University Press, 1991.

Ansell-Pearson, Keith. *Nietzsche Contra Rousseau*. Cambridge: Cambridge University Press, 1991.

Baczko, Bronislaw. "Rousseau et l'aliénation sociale." In *Annales de la Société Jean-Jacques Rousseau*. Librairie Armand Colin, 1962.

Berman, Marshall. *All That Is Solid Melts Into Air*. New York: Penguin Books, 1988.

Bloom, Allan. "Introduction" to Jean-Jacques Rousseau, *Emile, or On Education*. New York: Basic Books, 1979.

———. "Rousseau—The Turning Point." In *Confronting the Constitution*. Edited by Allan Bloom. Washington, DC: The AEI Press, 1990

Cassirer, Ernst. *The Question of Jean-Jacques Rousseau*. Edited and translated by Peter Gay. New Haven: Yale University Press, 1989.

Cohen, Ira H. *Ideology and Unconsciousness*. New York: New York University Press, 1982.

Colletti, Lucio. *From Rousseau to Lenin*. New York: Monthly Review Press, 1972.

Connoly, William E. *Political Theory and Modernity*. Oxford: Basil Blackwell, Ltd., 1988.

Dannhauser, Werner, J. "The Problem of the Bourgeois." In *The Legacy of Rousseau*. Edited by Clifford Orwin and Nathan Tarcov. Chicago: University of Chicago Press, 1997.

della Volpe, Galvano. *Rousseau and Marx*. London: Lawrence and Wishart, 1978.

Dent, N. J. H. *Rousseau: An Introduction to His Psychological, Social, and Political Theory*. New York: Basil Blackwell, Ltd., 1989.

———. *A Rousseau Dictionary*. Oxford: Blackwell Publishers, 1992.

Derathé, Robert. *Rousseau et la science politique de son temps*. Paris: Presses Universitaires de France, 1970.

Edwards, Paul. *The Encyclopedia of Philosophy*. New York: The MacMillan Company and The Free Press, 1967.

Ferrara, Alesandro. *Modernity and Authenticity*. Albany: State University of New York Press, 1993.

Feuer, Lewis. "What is Alienation? The Career of a Concept." *New Politics*, 1962.

Feuerlicht, Ignace. *Alienation: From the Past to the Future*. Westport, CT: Greenwood Press, 1978.

Gauthier, David. *Rousseau: The Sentiment of Existence*. Cambridge: Cambridge University Press, 2006.

Glenn, Gary D. "Inalienable Rights and Locke's Argument for Limited Government: Political Implications of a Right of Suicide." *Journal of Politics*, 46 (1984): 80–105.

Grant, Ruth W. *John Locke's Liberalism*. Chicago: University of Chicago Press, 1987.

———. *Hypocrisy and Integrity*. Chicago: University of Chicago Press, 1997.

Green, F. C. *Rousseau and the Idea of Progress*. Oxford: Clarendon Press, 1970.

Grotius, Hugo. *The Rights of War and Peace*. Edited and translated by A. C. Campbell, A. M. London: M. Walter Dunne Publishers, 1901.

———. *De Jure Belli Ac Pacis* [The Law of War and Peace], vol. 2. Edited and translated by Francis W. Kelsey. Oxford: Clarendon Press, 1925.

———. *De Jure Praedae Commentarius* [Commentary on the Law of Prize and Booty], vol. 2. Edited and translated by G. L. Williams and W. H. Zeydel. Oxford: Clarendon Press, 1950.

―――. *Prolegomena to the Law of War and Peace*. Edited by Edward Dumbauld. Translated by Francis W. Kelsey. New York: Liberal Arts Press, 1957.

―――. *The Freedom of the Seas*. Edited by James Brown Scott. Translated by Ralph Van Deman Magoffin. New York: Oxford University Press, 1972.

―――. *The Jurisprudence of Holland*. Edited and translated by Robert Warden Lee. Darmstadt, Germany: Scientia Verlag Aalen, 1977.

Hobbes, Thomas. *Man and Citizen* [De Homine and De Cive], edited by Bernard Gert. Indianapolis: Hackett Publishing Company, 1991.

―――. *Leviathan*. Edited by Edwin Curley. Indianapolis: Hackett, 1994.

Horowitz, Asher. *Rousseau, Nature, and History*. Toronto: University of Toronto Press. 1987.

Kelly, Christopher. "Rousseau and the Case Against (and for) the Arts." *The Legacy of Rousseau*. Edited by Clifford Orwin and Nathan Tarcov. Chicago:University of Chicago Press, 1997.

Kautz, Steven. "Privacy and Community." In *The Legacy of Rousseau*. Edited by Clifford Orwin and Nathan Tarcov. Chicago: University of Chicago Press, 1997.

Levine, Andrew. *The General Will: Rousseau, Marx, Communism*. Cambridge: Cambridge University Press, 1993.

Locke, John. *Two Treatises of Civil Government*. Edited by W. S. Carpenter. London: J. M. Dent & Sons, Ltd., 1955.

―――. *An Essay Concerning Human Understanding*. Vol. I. Edited by Alexander Campbell Fraser. New York: Dover, 1959.

―――. *Second Treatise of Government*. Edited by C. B. Macpherson. Indianapolis: Hackett, 1980.

Löwith, Karl. *From Hegel to Nietzsche*. Translated by David E. Green. New York: Holt, Rinehart and Winston, 1964.

Marcuse, Herbert. *One-Dimensional Man*. Boston: Beacon Press, 1964

Marks, Jonathan. *Perfection and Disharmony in the Thought of Jean-Jacques Rousseau*. New York: Cambridge University Press, 2005.

Marx, Karl, and Friedrich Engels. *Manifesto of the Communist Party*. *The Marx-Engels Reader*. Edited by Robert C. Tucker. New York: W. W. Norton & Company, Inc, 1978.

Marx, Karl. *Economic and Philosophic Manuscripts of 1844*. *The Marx-Engels Reader*. Edited by Robert C. Tucker. New York: W. W. Norton & Company, Inc., 1978.

―――. *The German Ideology: Part I*. In *The Marx-Engels Reader*. Edited by Robert C. Tucker. New York: W. W. Norton & Company, Inc., 1978.

―――. *Grundrisse*. London: Penguin Classics, 1973.

Masters, Roger D. *The Political Philosophy of Rousseau*. Princeton: Princeton University Press, 1968.

Melzer, Arthur M. "Rousseau and the Problem of Bourgeois Society." *American Political Science Review* 74 (1980):1018–1033.

―――. *The Natural Goodness of Man*. Chicago: University of Chicago Press. 1990.

―――. "Rousseau and the Modern Cult of Sincerity." *The Legacy of Rousseau*. Edited by Clifford Orwin and Nathan Tarcov. Chicago: University of Chicago Press, 1997.

Miller, James. *Rousseau: Dreamer of Democracy*. New Haven: Yale University Press, 1984.

Morgenstern, Mira. *Rousseau and the Politics of Ambiguity: Self, Culture and Society*. University Park: The Pennsylvania State University Press, 1996.

Meyers, Diana T. *Inalienable Rights: A Defense*. New York: Columbia University Press, 1985.

Neuhouser, Frederick. *Rousseau's Theodicy of Self-Love*. Oxford: Oxford University Press, 2008.

Ollman, Bertel. *Alienation*. Cambridge: Cambridge University Press, 1977.

Plattner, Marc F. *Rousseau's State of Nature*. DeKalb: Northern Illinois University Press, 1979.

Polin, Raymond. "The Rights of Man in Hobbes and Locke." *Political Theory and the Rights of Man.* Edited by D. D. Raphael. Bloomington: Indiana University Press, 1967.

Rapaczynski, Andrzej. *Nature and Politics: Liberalism in the Philosophies of Hobbes, Locke and Rousseau.* Ithaca: Cornell University Press, 1987.

Rousseau, Jean-Jacques. *Discourse on the Sciences and Arts. The First and Second Discourses.* Edited and translated by Roger D. Masters and Judith R. Masters. New York: St. Martin's Press, 1964.

―――. *Discourse on the Origin and Foundations of Inequality.* In *The First and Second Discourses.* Edited and translated by Roger D. Masters and Judith R. Masters. New York: St. Martin's Press, 1964.

―――. *Emile or On Education.* Translated by Allan Bloom. New York: Basic Books, 1979.

―――. *Oeuvres complètes.* Edited by Bernard Gagnebin and Marcel Raymond. 5 vols. Paris: Gallimard, Bibliothèque de la Pléiade, 1959–.

―――. *The Social Contract.* Translated by G. D. H. Cole. Amherst, NY: Prometheus Books, 1988.

―――. *Essay on the Origin of Languages.* In *The First and Second Discourses and Essay on the Origin of Languages.* Edited and translated by Victor Gourevitch. New York: Harper & Row Publishers, 1990.

―――. *Final Reply. Discourse on the Sciences and Arts and Polemics.* Edited and translated by Judith R. Bush, Roger D. Masters, and Christopher Kelly. Hanover, NH: University Press of New England, 1992.

―――. *Observations by Jean-Jacques Rousseau of Geneva* (Reply to the King of Poland). In *Discourse on the Sciences and Arts and Polemics.* Edited and translated by Judith R. Bush, Roger D. Masters and Christopher Kelly. Hanover, NH: University Press of New England, 1992.

―――. *Preface to Narcissus: Or the Lover of Himself. Discourse on the Sciences and Arts and Polemics.* Edited and translated by Judith R. Bush, Roger D. Masters and Christopher Kelly. Hanover, NH: University Press of New England, 1992.

Schaff, Adam. *Alienation as a Social Phenomenon.* Oxford: Pergamon Press, 1980.

Shklar, Judith N. *After Utopia: The Decline of Political Faith.* Princeton: Princeton University Press, 1957.

―――. *Men and Citizens.* Cambridge: Cambridge University Press, 1969.

―――. "Jean-Jacques Rousseau and Equality." *Daedalus* 107:3 (1978):13-25.

Simmons, A. John. *The Lockean Theory of Rights.* Princeton: Princeton University Press, 1992.

―――. *On the Edge of Anarchy: Locke, Consent, and the Limits of Society.* Princeton: Princeton University Press, 1993.

Starobinski, Jean. *Jean-Jacques Rousseau: Transparency and Obstruction.* Translated by Arthur Goldhammer. Chicago: University of Chicago Press, 1988.

Strong, Tracy B. *The Idea of Political Theory.* Notre Dame: University of Notre Dame Press, 1990.

Todorov, Tzvetan. *Frail Happiness: An Essay on Rousseau.* Translated by John T. Scott and Robert D. Zaretsky. University Park: The Pennsylvania State University Press, 2001.

Tuck, Richard. *Natural Rights Theories: Their Origin and Development.* Cambridge: Cambridge University Press, 1979.

Tully, James H. A *Discourse on Property: John Locke and His Adversaries.* Cambridge: Cambridge University Press, 1980.

Wiener, Philip P. *Dictionary of the History of Ideas.* New York: Charles Scribner's Sons. 1973–1974.

Yack, Bernard. *The Longing for Total Revolution.* Berkeley: University of California Press, 1992.

Index

About the Author

Sally Howard Campbell is associate professor of political science at Concord University in Athens, West Virginia, where she has taught since 2003. She teaches courses in political theory, international relations, and constitutional law. She received her master's degree from Rice University and holds a PhD from the University of Houston. She has co-authored articles for *The Journal of Conflict Resolution*, and *The American Journal of Political Science*, and was a contributor to *The Constitutionalism of the American States* (2008).